Redemption to Transformation

The Journey of Lent and Easter

*Cycle B Second Lesson Sermons for
Lent and Easter*

Richard Gribble, CSC

CSS Publishing Company, Inc.
Lima, Ohio

REDEMPTION TO TRANSFORMATION:
THE JOURNEY OF LENT AND EASTER
CYCLE B SECOND LESSON SERMONS FOR LENT AND EASTER

FIRST EDITION
Copyright © 2017
by CSS Publishing Co., Inc.

Library of Congress Cataloging-in-Publication Data

Gribble, Richard, author.
Title: Redemption to transformation : the journey of Lent and Easter : Cycle B
second lesson sermons for Lent and Easter / Richard Gribble, CSC.
Description: FIRST EDITION. | Lima, OH : CSS Publishing Company, Inc.,
2017.
Identifiers: LCCN 2017009717| ISBN 9780788028878 (pbk. : alk. paper) | ISBN
0788028871 (pbk.) Subjects: LCSH: Lenten sermons. | Lent--Sermons. | Eas-
ter--Sermons. | Church year sermons. | Common lectionary (1992). Year B. Clas-
sification: LCC BV4277 .G754 2017 | DDC 252/.62--dc23

For more information about CSS Publishing Company resources, visit our web-
site at www.csspub.com, email us at csr@csspub.com, or call (800) 241-4056.

e-book:
ISBN-13: 978-0-7880-2889-2
ISBN-10: 0-7880-2889-8

ISBN-13: 978-0-7880-2887-8
ISBN-10: 0-7880-2887-1   PRINTED IN USA

As a Christian my certain belief is that I have been redeemed by the Paschal mystery, the passion, death, and resurrection of Jesus Christ. Along the road of my Christian life I have been blessed with many experiences of transformation, but certainly the most powerful have come from encounters with people. It is appropriate, therefore, that this book be dedicated to a central person of my spiritual transformation, my dear friend Sister Tanl'a Santander Atauchi, CDP.

Table of Contents

Introduction

The Christian community celebrates God's love and the message of salvation throughout the liturgical year. Our annual cycle begins with the great anticipatory period of Advent. The community prepares for the Feast of the Incarnation by reflecting upon the hope of Christ's Second Coming and recalling the historic preparations for the Messiah's coming to our world through the heraldry of John the Baptist. The Christmas season, which follows sets our course for the remainder of the year, most of which is celebrated as the Season of Pentecost (Ordinary Time in the Roman Catholic tradition). The period of Pentecost is interrupted, however, several weeks after Christmas with two contiguous seasons, Lent and Easter, which prepare the community for and celebrate its salvation through the Paschal Mystery, the passion, death, and resurrection of Jesus Christ. The seasons of Lent and Easter are, therefore a critical period for the Christian to re-think and, as might be necessary, rebuild one's relationship with God. It is a special season of grace given us by God; we must wholly and faithfully participate and give thanks for the opportunities this time affords, personally and for the Christian faithful collectively.

Lent, the first of these two seasons, serves as a significant period of serious preparation for the celebration of Easter. The second lesson passages used during Liturgical Cycle B reflect what the church considers most important in this special journey. We must realize that at the outset of our journey a decision must be made — will we chose God or the world? While the latter is certainly the option of contemporary society, the Christian must choose God, for it is only through God that we can hope to stay on the road that leads to our immediate goal of Easter and our ultimate dream of salvation and eternal life. Assuming that we do choose God, then we must understand the need to be converted to the Christian message so that we can make a better effort to see things through the eyes of God and not our own, even though we might foolishly think we know best. Lent teaches us that Jesus is the one who will cure our spiritual blindness and release us from the chains, often self-imposed, that hold us prisoner. As our preparation enters Holy Week we learn of our need to walk the road with the Lord and to share his pain, as he bore our infirmities, although he had done nothing wrong. We must recall Saint Peter's words, "By his wounds you have been healed" (1 Peter 2:24). Finally, we must fully understand that there is a price to pay to experience God's glory; we must learn of our need to be cut down in order to discover our true path, the one that leads not to worldly success, but to the eternal life which is God's gift to all who believe.

If the Lenten journey is traversed successfully, then we can fully enter into the celebratory time of Easter. Yet, even as we observe these events we must acknowledge that the challenges of the Christian life are ever present. We should never forget British writer G.K. Chesterton's admonition in *What's Wrong with the World* (1910), "The Christian life has not been tried and found wanting; it has been found difficult and left untried." The Easter season reminds us that despite the triumph of Christ there will always be challenges to our belief. We seemingly cannot believe unless we see; yet we know that faith often is beyond proof and, thus, beyond sight as well. We are also challenged to discover ways of transforming problematic situations and what appears to be defeat into triumph through the grace of God. Additionally, this great season of grace teaches us that we must continually evaluate what we do and keep our eyes fixed on Christ and his mission and message. Finally, as Jesus ascends to the Father, we come to realize that the Lord's work in not complete and, therefore, each day presents us with the opportunity to do something to complete the master's work.

These sermons represent my understanding of the challenges presented us through this highly significant and very special journey. The church in its wisdom gives us this opportunity annually to review where we are and, after ascertaining our present position, the challenge to move to higher realms that are more consistent with our common Christian call to holiness. It is my hope that these reflections will be helpful to you as together we travel the path from Lent to Easter, and eventually to Christ and eternal life.

— Rev. Richard Gribble, CSC, Ph.D.

Ash Wednesday
2 Corinthians 5:20b-6:10

Be Reconciled with the Lord

We beseech you on behalf of Christ, be reconciled to God. For our sake he made him to be sin who knew no sin, so that in him we might become the righteousness of God. Working together with him, then, we entreat you not to accept the grace of God in vain. For he says, "At the acceptable time I have listened to you, and helped you on the day of salvation." Behold, now is the acceptable time; behold, now is the day of salvation. We put no obstacle in any one's way, so that no fault may be found with our ministry, but as servants of God we commend ourselves in every way: through great endurance, in afflictions, hardships, calamities, beatings, imprisonments, tumults, labors, watching, hunger; by purity, knowledge, forbearance, kindness, the Holy Spirit, genuine love, truthful speech, and the power of God; with the weapons of righteousness for the right hand and for the left; in honor and dishonor, in ill repute and good repute. We are treated as impostors, and yet are true; as unknown, and yet well known; as dying, and behold we live; as punished, and yet not killed; as sorrowful, yet always rejoicing; as poor, yet making many rich; as having nothing, and yet possessing everything.

Two brothers who lived on adjoining farms developed a bitter dispute. It was their first serious rift in forty years of farming side-by-side, sharing machinery, and trading labor and goods as necessary. They had never had a quarrel until now. It began with a small misunderstanding but eventually mushroomed into a major difference, and finally exploded into a war of words, followed by separation and silence. One morning there was a knock at the back door of the elder brother's door. He opened the door and found a man standing outside. He was stooped and was holding a carpenter's toolbox. "I am looking for a few day's work," said the itinerant carpenter. "Perhaps you have some small jobs that I can do." "Well, I believe I do," said the older brother. "Look across the creek at that other farm. That is my neighbor, in fact my brother's property. Last week there was a meadow between our farms, but then he ran a bulldozer through the river levee and now there is a creek between us. I suspect he did that to spite me, but I will do him one better. You see that big pile of lumber. I want you to build a fence, an eight-foot high fence, between us so that I never have to look at his place again. Can you handle such a job?" The man replied, "I think I understand the situation. Please show me your tool shed and I will do a job that will please you."

The brother was going to town, so he got the carpenter all set up and then left for the day. The carpenter toiled all day, measuring, cutting, and pounding nails. At sunset the brother returned from town just as the carpenter was finishing. The brother was aghast; there was no fence but rather a bridge across the creek. It was a terrific piece of workmanship, even including handrails. And to the older brother's surprise he saw his younger brother crossing the bridge with his arms outstretched. "You are quite a craftsman and brother to do this after all that was said between us." The two brothers warmly embraced at the center of the bridge. As they turned they saw the carpenter packing up his tools. "No wait," they said, "Don't leave. We have other projects for you to do." "No thanks," said the carpenter. I must be moving along. I have other bridges that need to be built."

The moral of the story is obvious. Sin destroyed the relationship between the brothers, but reconciliation in the form of the bridge builder restored the trust and confidence that was shattered. This story serves as an excellent entrée to the season of Lent that begins today on Ash Wednesday. The journey of Lent, this forty-day period of fasting, prayer, and almsgiving, begins, as we hear Saint Paul so clearly describe in writing to the Christian community at Corinth, with our need to be reconciled, within our own person, with others, and most assuredly and primarily with God. The apostle to the Gentiles certainly knew about reconciliation from his own experience. We must recall that he was transformed by the power of Christ from one who with great fervor and zeal sought to wipe out Christianity, into the evangelist who would bring Christ's message of love and peace to Gentile peoples throughout the Eastern Mediterranean world. As Paul himself wrote, he considered himself "the least of the apostles," one as he speaks "born abnormally" (1 Corinthians 15:8-9), yet called by God to dramatically change course in life and follow Jesus. He believed that if God could forgive him for all the ways that he had sought to destroy the church, then most assuredly God could forgive anyone.

Saint Paul understood that the greatness of God's reconciliation, like the itinerant carpenter could see the need for forgiveness between the two brothers. Thus, he writes, "We entreat you on behalf of Christ, be reconciled to God" (2 Corinthians 5:20b). Paul understood that the challenge for the Corinthians, and all of the fledgling Christian communities he founded, was great. Living as Christians in the pagan Roman world was a difficult task and many times individuals would fall into the trap of the societal norms. Thus, reconciling oneself to the Lord was an essential element of being a true disciple. He also understood that there was no need to wait, but applying our contemporary adage, "If something is worth doing it's worth doing now," he exhorted the Corinthians to seek reconciliation with God for it was both the acceptable time and the day of their salvation.

Paul also realized and instructed the Corinthians that reconciliation and the general life of discipleship would lead to and even require a certain amount of suffering. Again, Paul knew from personal experience that afflictions, hardships, imprisonments, sleepless nights, even being treated as an imposter would be the lot of those courageous enough to follow Jesus. But he equally knew that if we hold out, if we continue to walk the road with Christ, in the end we will reign with him (2 Timothy 2:12).

The challenge that Paul brings to the Corinthians is the same for us today. Lent has begun and we must start this great journey of faith by returning to the Lord, being reconciled, yet understanding that the process will not be easy. Reconciliation, however, must begin with oneself. Too often people cannot forgive themselves for things they have done, either to themselves or to others. A sense of low self-esteem absorbs many, trapping them within the confines of their own person. Such an inability to free oneself and be forgiven stunts the process of reconciliation before it can ever fully develop. Thus, we must begin the journey of reconciliation by admitting our inadequacies and sinfulness and not allowing them to drag us down, hold us back, or impede us from the road that reconciliation requires.

Next, we must learn to be reconciled with others. We have hurt others; others have hurt us. We all know deep down that holding a grudge against another is inconsistent with our Christian call. Moreover, it brings us no positive result. Jesus puts it very plainly when he tells us that before we offer our gift at the altar we must be reconciled with our brother (Matthew 5:24). The inability to forgive others is like a ball and chain around the leg of a prisoner; it impedes our ability to move forward. We must cut the chain, seek forgiveness, and then move forward. Reconciliation with our brother works in the opposite direction as well; we need to be forgiven by others. This process can only begin, however, when we admit our error. Sin is part of life, but if we can admit our faults and mistakes, and be reconciled, we demonstrate the kind of person Christ calls us to be.

Lastly, and most importantly, we must find reconciliation with God. All of us are sinners. God understands this for we were made as incomplete human beings needing reconciliation from Christ. We cannot run away or think that in some way the Lord is not aware of the things we have done or failed to do. If we think this for a moment, the only person we are kidding is ourselves. The Lord does not demand perfection, but he does require us to give our best effort that must mean in part that we realize our need to be reconciled, to ask forgiveness from God who is full of mercy. Nothing we have done or failed to do can keep us from the loving and forgiving embrace of the Lord. Interestingly and certainly significantly, in the New Testament the only person who was guaranteed a place in the heavenly kingdom with Jesus was the thief crucified alongside him who asked for forgiveness. Jesus told him, "This day you will be with me in paradise" (Luke 23:43). If Jesus can forgive and grant salvation to a criminal at the hour of his death, if he can use the talents of one like Paul, who so zealously persecuted the faith, to evangelize the nations, then assuredly the Lord can and will extend the hand of forgiveness and reconciliation to us.

Thus, as we begin this sacred time of Lent, let us listen to the message of Saint Paul and be reconciled to the Lord. There's no need to wait, for Jesus is eagerly waiting with his arms outstretched on the cross for us to accept his loving embrace and forgiveness.

Suffering Leads to Victory

*For Christ also died for sins once for all, the righteous for the
unrighteous, that he might bring us to God, being put to death
in the flesh but made alive in the spirit; in which he went and
preached to the spirits in prison, who formerly did not obey, when
God's patience waited in the days of Noah, during the building of
the ark, in which a few, that is, eight persons, were saved through
water. Baptism, which corresponds to this, now saves you, not as a
removal of dirt from the body but as an appeal to God for a clear
conscience, through the resurrection of Jesus Christ.*

The Comanche people moaned aloud to the Great Spirit:
"O Great Spirit, our land is dying and we are dying too. Tell
us what we have done wrong to make you so angry. End
this terrible drought and save your people before we perish
altogether. Tell us what we must do so that once more you
will send rain and restore our land to life." For three days the
people prayed and danced, they prayed and danced, but no
rain came.

When the rain did not come, the elders of the tribe went
to the hills to listen to the wind that carried the voice of the
Great Spirit. After a few days they returned and the people
gathered to hear their message. The elders solemnly proclaimed, "The Great Spirit says that the people have become
selfish. For years they have taken from the earth but not giv-
en anything back. So the Great Spirit says that we must sacrifice taking the burnt offering of our most valuable possession and scattering its ashes on the winds to the four corners

of the earth. When this sacrifice is completed, rain will come and life will return to the earth.

The people were grateful to the Great Spirit for telling them what they must do and they went back to their tepees to look for their most valued possession. One warrior said, I am sure the Great Spirit does not want my prize bow. One woman suggested, "I know the Great Spirit does not want my special blanket." And so it went throughout the village; everyone had an excuse to keep what he or she valued most.

Among the few children who had not died from hunger was a little girl named She-Who-Sits-Alone. In her tepee she said to herself. "O Great Spirit, it is my warrior doll that you want. It is the only possession I have left of my parents. The doll had a belt made of bone and beaded leggings. On its head were blue feathers matching the sky. She knew what she had to do. Later that night when everyone was asleep, She-Who-Sits-Alone crawled out from her blanket, took a lighted stick from the campfire and went to the top of the mountain. There she placed the lighted stick on the ground and spoke, "Great Spirit, here is my warrior doll. It is the only thing I have from my mother and father. It is my most prized possession; please accept it." Holding the doll, she gathered some twigs and fanned up a fire and held her doll near it. While she was sad and suffered for her loss, she thought of her parents and grandparents and friends who had died from hunger and thus thrust the doll into the fire.

When the flames died down and the ashes cooled, she scooped them up and scattered them to the four winds. Exhausted after her effort, she fell asleep without her doll but with a smile on her face. The next morning the rising sun woke her. She sat up and looked out over the hill. As far as she could see, where her doll's ashes had fallen, the ground was covered with beautiful blue flowers like little bluebonnets. They were as blue as the feathers on her doll's feathers.

When the people came out of their tepees they could hardly believe their eyes. They ran to the mountain where She-Who-Sits-Alone was gazing upon the wonderful site. There was no doubt in their minds; the flowers were a sign from the Great Spirit that they were forgiven. Thus, they sang and danced and thanked the Great Spirit and as they did a gentle rain began to fall. The land began to live again and the people were saved.

This classic Native American story of the origins of the bluebonnet presents a powerful theme of the willingness of one to suffer so that good, and in the end triumph, can be achieved. As the Christian community begins to enter more fully and deeply into the season of Lent on this first Sunday, Saint Peter writing to the nascent followers of Jesus, speaks of this same powerful idea.

If there was anyone who was transformed by the power of Christ's resurrection it was Peter. If you read the gospels, Peter is often shown to have a lack of understanding. He rejects the need for Jesus to suffer immediately after the Lord declares him to be the rock upon which he will build the church, and most sadly, he denied Jesus three times on the morning of the crucifixion when the Lord needed him most. Yet, as the Acts of the Apostles shows very clearly, Peter is a completely transformed individual in the wake of the resurrection. He boldly proclaims his faith and is completely undeterred by threats from the Jewish religious elite who order him to cease his preaching about Jesus.

It is this renewed and transformed Peter about whom we hear in our reading this week. He speaks to the fledgling Christian community by drawing a comparison between its suffering and that of Christ. As Jesus triumphed over death through his resurrection, so will they. Peter tells them that baptism is their pledge of this triumph for it gives them a share in the Lord's resurrection. The apostle makes an additional connection with the Old Testament figure of Noah. As he and his family were saved by passage through the waters of the flood, so Christians will be saved by their passage through the waters of baptism.

The suffering that the Christian community endured during the apostolic period and beyond was overcome by the faith and fidelity of the people. They took to heart the words of Peter in today's reading; they believed that Christ's suffering and death, as terrible and tragic as it was, led to a positive result. Thus, they could he confident that they, like Jesus and Peter, could boldly live their new faith in word and action, confident that in the end it would bring triumph for themselves and the community of faith. Christians today owe a debt of gratitude to these great men and women of faith, for it is upon their shoulders that we stand; it is their faith, courage and willingness to suffer that allow the Christian message to spread throughout the world.

The obvious question for us in our first world, generally comfortable existence is, how much are willing to suffer for our faith? We all know that suffering will come our way, whether we want it or not. Personal suffering through ill health, economic problems, broken relationships, or family difficulties are part of life; we suffer as well when people we know and love face similar challenges in their lives. We do not need to seek suffering, for it will come our way; it is indeed part of life. It is natural to avoid people, situations, or even possibilities that we know may be problematic, hurtful, or bring suffering, but when it comes to our faith should there be another approach or standard we use? Contemporary life, especially in the Western first-world environment in which we live, exalts ideas and promotes actions and ways of thinking that violate the basic precepts of Jesus as outlined by the gospel evangelists and the other New Testament authors. It is easy to follow the path of the majority to walk the easy, unencumbered trouble-free path. But as Jesus reminds us in his Sermon on the Mount: "Enter through the narrow gate;

for the gate is wide and the road is easy that leads to destruction, and there are many who take it. For the gate is narrow and the road is hard that leads to life, and there are few who find" (Matthew 7:13-14).

The challenge for Christians today is not to seek to suffer for our faith, but rather when suffering is required to profess and uphold the things we believe, but to not shy away, hold back, or shirk our responsibility as baptized followers of Jesus Christ. Christianity, if lived well, especially in today's society, will require us to suffer. It may be the loss of a friend or opportunity, rejection by a colleague at work or a neighbor down the street, or even having our opinion on other matters placed on the sidelines, with our religious beliefs, as irrelevant, outdated or even not applicable. Jesus warned us on numerous occasions that being one of his followers would not be easy. Rather, he made it very clear that being rejected or even hated by others could easily be our lot. He summarized all the possible negative effects of being a member of the church when he said, "If any want to become my followers, let them deny themselves and take up their cross and follow me. For those who want to save their life will lose it, and those who lose their life for my sake will find it" (Matthew 16:24-25).

The season of Lent presents us the challenge to ask how much are we willing to suffer in order that the message of Christ be proclaimed? In the Native American story of the bluebonnet, She-Who-Sits-Alone was willing to suffer by sacrificing her warrior doll so that rain would return to the earth and restore the life and vitality of her people. She did not seek to suffer, but realized that it was necessary if the end for which she and her people had prayed and danced so long, could ever be achieved. The Great Spirit demanded sacrifice and the young girl was willing to do what was necessary for her people. What about all of us? Saint Peter's comparison of Christ's suffering to that of the Christian community of his day is equally present in the twenty-first century. But let us always remember that great suffering brings great triumph. The powerful Legend of the Thorn Bird drives homes this message:

There is a legend about a bird that sings just once in its life, more sweetly than any creature on the face of the earth. From the moment it leaves the nest it searches for a thorn tree, and does not rest until it has found one. Then, singing among the savage branches, it impales itself upon the longest, sharpest spine. And, as it suffers and dies, it rises above its own agony to sing more beautifully than the lark or nightingale. One great superlative song is its price for existence. But the whole world still listens and God in the heaven smiles. For the best is only brought about at the cost of great pain.

May we be found worthy of the challenge, rise to the occasion, and be willing to suffer for our faith. If we do not suffer in some measure for our faith these days, then most likely we are not fulfilling the expectation of Christ. Let us, therefore, go forward and live our faith boldly and proclaim it widely and loudly. God is expecting great things of us, let us not disappoint him.

Lent 2
Romans 4:13-25

Enduring the Trials of Faith

The promise to Abraham and his descendants, that they should inherit the world, did not come through the law but through the righteousness of faith. If it is the adherents of the law who are to be the heirs, faith is null and the promise is void. For the law brings wrath, but where there is no law there is no transgression.

That is why it depends on faith, in order that the promise may rest on grace and be guaranteed to all his descendants — not only to the adherents of the law but also to those who share the faith of Abraham, for he is the father of us all, as it is written, "I have made you the father of many nations" — in the presence of the God in whom he believed, who gives life to the dead and calls into existence the things that do not exist. In hope he believed against hope, that he should become the father of many nations; as he had been told, "So shall your descendants be." He did not weaken in faith when he considered his own body, which was as good as dead because he was about a hundred years old, or when he considered the barrenness of Sarah's womb. No distrust made him waver concerning the promise of God, but he grew strong in his faith as he gave glory to God, fully convinced that God was able to do what he had promised. That is why his faith was "reckoned to him as righteousness." But the words, "it was reckoned to him," were written not for his sake alone, but for ours also. It will be reckoned to us who believe in him that raised from the dead Jesus our Lord, who was put to death for our trespasses and raised for our justification.

"In the seventh year of his reign, two days before his 65th birthday, in the presence of a full consistory of cardinals, Jean Marie Barette, Pope Gregory XVII signed an instrument of abdication, took off the fisherman's ring, handed his seal to the Cardinal Camerlengo and made a curt speech of farewell." So begins the power novel *The Clowns of God*, the second volume of a trilogy of tales about popes and faith written by Morris West, the Australian-born author. In the story the pope has seen a vision of the Second Coming. He feels that the message of Christ's return must be promulgated throughout the world. Therefore, he gathers his closest advisors, the curia and College of Cardinals, and asks their advice. They tell him that such a message cannot be published. "It will throw the world into a panic," they claim. The pope is confused but feels that he has only one alternative; he must be true to himself. Thus, he decides to abdicate his position. This he does, placing himself under the obedience of an abbot in a monastery outside of Rome.

After one week at the monastery, Jean Marie receives his first visitor. His name is Carl Mendelius, a longtime friend and former Jesuit priest, who now as a married man is teaching theology in a German university. The two friends speak and begin to map out a strategy whereby the message of Jean Marie's vision may be promulgated to the world.

The plan is foiled, however, before it can be enacted. Mendelius, working in Germany, is felled by a letter bomb sent by a would-be assassin just as he made ready to post the text of the message to a group of the world's scholars. Jean Marie, in England to give a speech where the message will be revealed, suffers a severe heart attack. As he clings to life in a London hospital, Jean Marie receives a strange visitor. The man is young, about thirty years old. He is tall, strong, and speaks with a Middle East accent, although his origin seems a mystery. He wears a beautiful and ancient ring which has inscribed on it the Christian symbol of a fish. This man calls himself Mr. Atha. The stranger tells Jean Marie that he must persevere but that the message which he feels must be told is already present if people will only recognize it.

Several weeks later Jean Marie returns to his native France to recuperate fully. One day he goes for a walk in a Parisian park. He sits down and observes the scene. There is a group of children playing nearby. They are a special group; they are mentally handicapped. In this experience Jean Marie begins to realize that the essential message of his vision is to accept God, to endure the trials of faith. He can see this in the unpretentious lives of these children whom he calls the "clowns of God."

Months later Jean Marie is present with his newfound friends, the clowns of God. They have gone to a remote mountain villa to celebrate the Christmas feast. To this isolated place, Mr. Atha comes quite unexpectedly. Jesus, the Christ, has returned as was predicted to claim his own. Jean Marie has endured the great trial of faith and discovered God in the process.

Morris West's epic novel demonstrates that we must persevere through the great trials of faith that come our way. In a similar way, Saint Paul writes to the Romans and speaks to them about the great faith of Abraham, suggesting to them, and by extension to Christians today, that persistence in faith is an absolute necessity to be a true follower of Jesus Christ.

The Judeo-Christian tradition of which we are all members rests upon the faith of Abram, the first patriarch. We recall the basic story as articulated in the book of Genesis. Abram (the original name of Abraham) was a wandering Aramean from the land of Ur. God came to him with an unbelievable story — that he would be the father of a great nation. He was told to leave his ancestral heritage and go to a new land that would become the home of this great nation. Paul reminds us that Abram was an old man who was childless and his wife, Sarah, was barren and beyond the age to give birth, yet somehow he continued to place his faith in God, believing in hope that the promises of God would one day be manifested in his life. Even after his son

Isaac was born, Abram, now with the new name of Abraham, was again asked to persevere through a great trial of faith when God asked him to sacrifice his one chance at progeny, his one opportunity to truly be the father of a great nation. Again, however, Abraham unhesitatingly went forward with every intention to sacrifice his son until God sent his angel to stay his hand promising, "Because you have done this, and have not withheld your son, your only son, I will indeed bless you, and I will make your offspring as numerous as the stars of heaven and the sand that is on the seashore" (Genesis 22:16b-17a).

Saint Paul's personal experience of faith and the need to persevere gives even greater credence to his words about Abraham. Paul, the great persecutor of the New Way of Jesus Christ became, through the power of his conversion, the great apostle to Gentiles. But Paul's faith was tested on numerous occasions. He suffered beatings and lashings and was even stoned by those who rejected his message. He was disowned by his own Jewish people. He suffered shipwreck and was forced into exile in defending himself to the emperor in Rome. Yet, it seems that the various trials only made Paul stronger and more determined in his discipleship; the more difficult things became the more fervent was his message and the stronger his faith.

The great faith and persistence of Jean Marie Barette in West's novel, and the examples of Abraham and Saint Paul, provide ample evidence of our need to persevere through the ups and downs and vicissitudes of our life, and to cling onto our faith in Jesus. The contemporary twenty-first century society in which we live tests our faith in varied ways on almost a daily basis. Since the dawn of civilization humanity has been tempted with power wealth and prestige, the same ideas that Satan unsuccessfully tried to get Jesus to grasp in his famous forty-day desert experience before the onset of his public ministry. Today we measure the success and unfortunately even at times the quality of people on the amount of power, wealth, and prestige they have accumulated. It's almost impossible to avoid at least one of these temptations each day. They at least sidetrack and at times even cause us to take detours in our spiritual life that draws away from our relationship with Christ. Thus, we need to persevere through these trials and have sufficient faith that if we continue on the less traveled, but nevertheless only proper road that leads to Christ, our faith in the end will be rewarded.

Faith is often tested by the unexpected events in our life, especially those with hurtful or tragic consequences. It is a test to, "keep your head on straight," if we achieve a windfall or some great accomplishment prompts us to concentrate on our own self achievement. Most of the time, however, it is the negative events that truly test our faith. Unexpected and/or untimely loss of a job or severe economic decline, might prompt us to seek easy or possibly unethical answers to our dilemma. Sudden illness, incapacity, or even death to a family member or friend often leaves us so stunned we are totally uncertain where to go or what to say or do. Trials of faith present themselves in our spiritual life as well. We pray for certain things, whether it be the health and prosperity of someone we know, the answer to a difficult dilemma, or hundreds of other possible needs and desires. We become frustrated, however, when the answer that we desire does not come in the time frame we want or need. We think that God is not listening, that he is too busy or even unconcerned. We never consider the possibility that the answer the Lord gives might be different than what we want. But we must believe that Christ is not only listening, but answers our prayers, for as he stated in his famous Sermon on the Mount: "Ask, it will be given you; search, and you will find; knock, and the door will be opened for you. For everyone who asks receives, and everyone who searches finds, and everyone who knocks, the door will be opened (Matthew 7:7-8). Placing faith in God seems so inadequate because we have absolutely no control on the Lord's response. Thus, we look for the easier, more common, and certainly tangible human answer.

Although such a response is very common and a natural human reaction, it cannot be the proper response of one who bears the name Christian. No, as Saint Paul so clearly states, faith must be the central core of our relationship with Jesus. Our faith will constantly be tested, but as the trials that beset Abraham and Paul made them stronger and better able to deal with future difficulties, so too negotiating our faith challenges will make us better, stronger, and more able to endure. Jesus never promised that being a Christian would be an easy road. On the contrary, he very clearly stated that the exact opposite would be the case. "If any want to become my followers, let them deny themselves and take up their cross and follow me. For those who want to save their life will lose it, and those who lose their life for my sake will find it" (Matthew 16:24b-25).

Jean Marie Barette grew into the knowledge that God was sending him a significant trial that needed to be negotiated. His willingness to be true to himself and persevere, despite the difficulties he faced, demonstrated his acceptance of his trial. Similarly, Abraham, about whom Saint Paul writes, and the apostle himself also demonstrated that efficacious faith requires perseverance. Let us, therefore, never give up on ourselves, on others, or especially on God. Let us realize that without our faith in God nothing is possible, but with faith in the Lord all things are possible. It is this faith, God's gift to us, that will help us in the trials and tribulations of this life, but more importantly bring us one day to eternal life with God.

Wisdom to the World,
but Foolishness to God

For the word of the cross is folly to those who are perishing, but to us who are being saved it is the power of God. For it is written, "I will destroy the wisdom of the wise, and the cleverness of the clever I will thwart." Where is the wise man? Where is the scribe? Where is the debater of this age? Has not God made foolish the wisdom of the world? For since, in the wisdom of God, the world did not know God through wisdom, it pleased God through the folly of what we preach to save those who believe. For Jews demand signs and Greeks seek wisdom, but we preach Christ crucified, a stumbling block to Jews and folly to Gentiles, but to those who are called, both Jews and Greeks, Christ the power of God and the wisdom of God. For the foolishness of God is wiser than men, and the weakness of God is stronger than men.

Students of American history have always been fascinated by the life and career of the sixteenth president of the United States, Abraham Lincoln. Honest Abe, as he was known by his Kentucky and Illinois peers, is the subject of history lessons from primary through graduate school education. Lincoln was the stereotypical backwoodsman who felt the call to public service of the state, on local and national levels. He became well known for his anti-slavery political and moral stance and saw his goal as president to preserve the Union. But few have ever looked carefully at the method he used to fulfill his call and meet his goal. His dedication and faithfulness to nation would override all feelings and past associations.

The historian and Pulitzer Prize winning author, Doris Kearns Goodwin, has in her book, *Team of Rivals: The Political Genius of Abraham Lincoln* demonstrated the path Lincoln used to preserve the Union, a path that could not have been easy, but it was the only course to best guarantee his goal of national unity, which for Lincoln was absolute. He would be faithful to the end; he would hold to his principles.

Professor Goodwin demonstrates how Lincoln brought together for his cabinet a team that on one level was the most unlikely combination, but on a second was absolutely the perfect team for the task at hand. In the 1860 Republican presidential nomination race, Lincoln was clearly the dark horse candidate. His rivals were all better known and possessed more experience: New York Senator William H. Seward, Ohio Governor Salmon P. Chase, and the distinguished elder statesman from Missouri, Edward Bates. All three had studied law, were great orators, and opposed slavery. Historians attribute Lincoln's nomination to chance. It is very interesting that when Lincoln took the oath of office he chose these men, his most ardent rivals, for the top spots in his cabinet: Seward was made Secretary of State, Chase made Secretary of the Treasury and Bates was appointed Attorney General. For the remaining top posts, Lincoln chose men from the other side of the political aisle, the Democratic camp: Gideon Welles was made Secretary of the Navy, Montgomery Blair was appointed Postmaster General, and Edwin Stanton, a man who detested Lincoln, but at his funeral referred to him as "a man for the ages," was made Secretary of War. Thus, Lincoln weaved together a team of rivals for his cabinet, all of whom were better known, better educated, and more experienced in public life. Because the goal, namely the preservation of the Union, was so critical, and completely consistent with his call, Abraham Lincoln chose the rough road, the road of faithfulness to the nation, the road of principle. Yes, Lincoln was a man of principle;

he did what was necessary to protect the nation he had taken an oath to serve.

On the surface, from what one might call a practical perspective, Lincoln's actions were certainly foolish. Why would a president invite one's enemies, including an individual who literally detested him and unjustly berated him in every way, to form the inner circle of trusted advisors who would assist him during such a critical moment in the nation's history? When Lincoln formed his cabinet, many thought he had made some serious errors, but history tells us that what seemed to be foolish to most, was actually the best choices for the country. Thus, Lincoln and his apparently "foolish actions" serve as an excellent metaphor for the clear message articulated by Saint Paul in writing to the Christian community at Corinth.

At first glance, the message of Paul to the Corinthians is foolish on a couple of different levels. First, since he was primarily speaking to Gentiles who were religiously formed with a pantheon of multiple gods and goddesses, the idea of monotheism was foreign, to say the least. But Paul's message was apparently foolish for another reason. This monotheistic God that Paul preached allowed himself to be crucified, a most humiliating and painful death. Why would an all-powerful God allow this? Paul could rightly say that for nonbelievers the cross was truly foolishness. Paul says that his message is a stumbling block to Jews and foolishness to Gentiles, but a source of wisdom to those who believe. But the great apostle to the Gentiles goes even further by saying that what appears to be foolishness on the part of God is actually wisdom which is greater than any human wisdom. The apparent weakness of God, in allowing Jesus to be crucified, is actually stronger than human strength. Paul's words to the people of Corinth were completely paradoxical; they appeared to be false but in actuality they were true.

The paradoxical nature of Paul's challenge is as true today as it was when he first wrote this letter. Jesus' actions, words, and message of love and peace which emphasized. Simplicity, fidelity, and commitment are, unfortunately, not of great value in our contemporary society, yet their veracity can never be questioned. The humble, the weak, the ordinary can teach us much, but contemporary society is not open to or ready to receive the message.

Yes, the values and goals of today's society, while generally accepted, can be foolishness to God. We live in a world that constantly battles with the temptations of power, wealth, and prestige. These have always been present to humanity and even Jesus was forced to endure them as described with great detail by Saint Matthew (4:1-11). When tempted to turn stones into bread, throw himself from the top of the temple, or worship Satan to obtain all the treasures of the world, Jesus turned the tables on evil and rejected all its allurements. What Jesus did might have seemed like foolishness to some, but it was a manifestation of the paradox that Paul addresses in today's lesson. People today are equally tempted as was Jesus in the desert, but things might be even more challenging now. In many ways society measures our value to the world and our success by the amount of power, wealth, and prestige we obtain. We are considered important if we hold positions of power, amass great wealth, and achieve worldly prestige for our accomplishments. Yet, if Paul is right and the great wisdom of the world is foolishness to God, then our society is moving in the wrong direction. If you read the daily paper, or listen to the news from radio or television, you do not often hear stories of humility, peace, fidelity, and commitment. Once in a while an individual act or one's life, like Mother Teresa of Calcutta, impresses sufficiently to be noticed, but unfortunately this is more the exception than the rule.

The world desires, exalts, and almost divinizes victory and accomplishment. The more degrees we obtain, triumphs we notch, and goals we achieve, the higher on the secular ladder of success we will climb. Points are not given for random acts of kindness, fidelity to individuals or principles, or commitment to a cause. Yet, these apparent "foolish actions" that seem to get us nowhere in society, are precisely what our Christian vocation calls us to do. While the world continually tells us how important it is to be noticed, gain wealth, and achieve high position, Jesus' message challenges us to seek humility and to live our lives for others. If we can follow Jesus' lead, then we will receive much. Christ made a promise to Peter and his other apostles when they worried that being his disciples and giving their lives would be too high a price to pay: "Everyone who has left houses or brothers or sisters or father or mother or children or fields, for my name's sake, will receive a hundredfold, and will inherit eternal life" (Matthew 19:29).

Those who were rational thinkers in the mid-nineteenth century truly believed that Abraham Lincoln's choices for his cabinet were foolish. Enemies and rivals could never, it seemed, be the proper choice for those who would guide the nation through its worst domestic crisis in history, the Civil War. Yet, history shows us that foolishness was proven to be great wisdom. In a similar way, Paul tells the Corinthians, and by extension, all of us, through the timelessness of Scripture, that the wisdom of the world then and now is foolishness in the eyes of God. It is easy and expedient to do what everyone else does, to follow the crowd, but to take the difficult and less utilized path is not easy but could indeed be the only proper way. A little story aptly challenges us to find the proper way, even when it might seem foolish.

Three businessmen from New York were in Chicago for a series of meetings. They all assured their spouses that they would be home in plenty of time for dinner on Friday. However, one thing led to the next and the meetings ran over time. As the businessmen raced through the airport, tickets in hand, hoping to catch their plane home, they inadvertently knocked over a table loaded with fruit. Without stopping two of them reached the plane in time and boarded with a sigh of relief. One man, realizing that in his rush he may have hurt someone or something, returned to the table with the overturned fruit. When he arrived he found a little ten year-old girl, who was selling the fruit, feeling about the floor in an effort to pick them up. The child was obviously blind. The salesman gathered up the fruit and noticed that several items were bruised. He reached into his wallet and gave the child $20 saying, "Please take this money for the damage we caused. I am very sorry for what we have done." The girl, although unable to see his face, called out, "Are you Jesus?" He responded, "Oh, my word, no." But she replied, "When I was on the floor searching for the fruit I prayed that Jesus would come and help me and you came." The businessman straightened up, and calmly walked toward the gate. His plane had just left.

Lent 4
Ephesians 2:1-10

Celebrating the Virtue of Humanity

And you he made alive, when you were dead through the trespasses and sins in which you once walked, following the course of this world, following the prince of the power of the air, the spirit that is now at work in the sons of disobedience. Among these we all once lived in the passions of our flesh, following the desires of body and mind, and so we were by nature children of wrath, like the rest of mankind. But God, who is rich in mercy, out of the great love with which he loved us, even when we were dead through our trespasses, made us alive together with Christ (by grace you have been saved), and raised us up with him, and made us sit with him in the heavenly places in Christ Jesus, that in the coming ages he might show the immeasurable riches of his grace in kindness toward us in Christ Jesus. For by grace you have been saved through faith; and this is not your own doing, it is the gift of God — not because of works, lest any man should boast. For we are his workmanship, created in Christ Jesus for good works, which God prepared beforehand, that we should walk in them.

Many years ago on one very bitterly cold evening in Northern Virginia, an older man waited for a ride across the Potomac River. The wait seemed endless; his body became numb and stiff from the frigid north wind. As he waited, he heard the faint steady rhythm of approaching horses. Anxiously he watched as several horsemen rounded the bend. He let the first one pass without an effort to get his attention. Then another passed by and still another. Finally, the last rider neared the spot where the old man sat like a statue of snow. As this last man drew near, the old man caught the rider's eye and said, "Sir, would you mind giving an old man a ride to the other side of the river? There doesn't seem to be a passageway by foot."

Bringing his horse to a stop, the rider replied, "Sure thing, sir. Hop on board." Seeing that the old man was unable to lift his half-frozen body from the ground, the horsemen dismounted and helped the old man onto the horse. The horsemen took the old man not just across the river, but to his destination which was just a few miles away. As they came near to the tiny, but cozy cottage, the horsemen's curiosity caused him to inquire, "Sir, I noticed that you let several other riders pass by without making an effort to secure a ride. Then I came and you immediately asked me for a ride. I'm curious why, on such a bitter winter night, you would wait and ask the last rider. What if I had refused and left you there?"

The older man lowered himself slowly down from the horse, looked the rider straight in the eyes and said, "I've been around these parts for some time. I reckon I know people pretty well. The man continued, "I looked into the eyes of the other riders and immediately saw there was no concern for my situation. It would have been useless even to ask them for a ride. But when I looked into your eyes, kindness and compassion and mercy were evident. I knew, then and there, that your gentle spirit would welcome the opportunity to give me assistance in my time of need.

The heartwarming comments touched the horseman deeply. He said, "I am grateful for what you have said. May I never get too busy in my own affairs that I fail to respond to the needs of others with kindness and compassion." With that, President Thomas Jefferson turned his horse around and made his way back to the White House.

This anecdote from the life of the third president of the United States speaks of humility, that virtue that helps us to understand that we are no better than anyone else that we are all created in the image and likeness of God and, therefore, equal in God's sight. Saint Paul, writing to the Christian community at Ephesus that he established during his second missionary journey, reminds these nascent followers of Jesus that they must be humble and compassionate as Jesus demonstrated mercy and humbled himself for them. Paul accurately describes the situation of how the Ephesians moved from the death of sin to a life in Christ as a result of Jesus' great act of humility. The people had lived a polytheistic existence, following the power of the world. Their day-to-day existence acknowledged nothing of the true God, but rather was guided by the passions and desires of the flesh. Yet, even when humanity was in the grasp of sin, Christ came among us, bringing the immeasurable riches of his love and allowing us to be saved by grace, not by what we do, but rather by the faith that we possess. Christ, although clearly above humanity in every conceivable way, nevertheless became incarnate in order to provide the one and only path that would lead us back to the Father. In his famous Philippians hymn, Paul articulated this idea very clearly: "Though he was in the form of God, he did not regard equality with God as something to be exploited, but emptied himself, taking the form of a slave, being born in human likeness. And being found in human form, he humbled himself and became obedient to the point of death — even death on a cross" (Philippians 2:6-7). Probably unknowingly, President Jefferson, when he picked up the old man and gave him a ride, was imitating the humility of Jesus. We are called to do likewise in our lives.

Humility has many facets, but three of the most important ideas, which form a sort of trinity, are compassion, forgiveness and reconciliation. Rather than exhibiting these three virtues, too often revenge and pride cloud our vision, not allowing us to humble ourselves sufficiently to find the reconciliation we need, within our own person, with others and, of course, with God. Our inability to let go of past hurts, clutching on to old grudges, and desiring revenge for what others have done to us are terrible realities that unfortunately often plague us. When we have been hurt by another we hold on to the pain as tenaciously as a wild animal clutches its prey; letting go, it seems, is not a possibility. Yet, experience, as the great teacher, suggests that our failure to release ourselves from the past only weighs us down, impeding our ability to move forward. As surely as in past times, when a ball and chain was placed on the leg of a prisoner to prevent him from escaping, so too holding grudges and refusing to let go of past hurts makes us prisoners, not allowing us to express compassion, find reconciliation, and move forward.

Jesus certainly never held a grudge. On the contrary, he sought to be reconciled even when he was on the cross. We must remember his words, "Father, forgive them; for they do not know what they are doing" (Luke 23:34a). An apocryphal yet illustrative story aptly describes the humility and forgiveness of Christ: It was the end of the world and all of the saints destined for heaven were climbing a ladder to the pearly gates. Jesus and Saint Peter were there to meet them. After the last person had reached heaven, Jesus, looking somewhat sad, continued to search down on the earth. This prompted Peter to ask, "Lord, who are you looking for?" Jesus responded, "I am looking for Judas; I was hoping he may have repented before he died."

The humility of compassion, mercy, and reconciliation that Jesus gives to us begins with removing old grudges and eliminating revenge from our hearts, but then the process moves to higher and deeper levels. Actually, compassion and mercy must begin with oneself. Low self-esteem is far too rampant in our contemporary society. People view themselves as insufficiently intelligent, attractive, athletic, or a host of other "necessary" attributes that contemporary society tells us are essential. Too often people cannot forgive themselves for actions or words in the past. Again, like the ball and chain on the prisoner's leg, we hold ourselves back.

Mercy and compassion must begin at home. When we look into the mirror we should see a child of God, created uniquely and special to carry out a vocation specifically chosen by the Lord for us. We need to release ourselves, strip away our self-imposed straitjacket, and be the people God has called us to be.

Once we have found compassion and reconciliation within ourselves, then we must forgive and show mercy to others. When we keep others at a distance, especially as a result of past experience, we limit ourselves and the potential of the other. Rather than concentrating on our past hurts or perceived inabilities, we should learn from the famous steel magnate and philanthropist, Andrew Carnegie, who once quipped, "I can see the golden nugget inside every person." We cannot erase our memories; we can do nothing about the past. We can, however, control the future with respect to our ideas and attitudes toward others.

Once we have humbled ourselves sufficiently and found compassion in our relationships with others, then we must move to the level of accepting the mercy of God. Jesus' whole life and message was centered on compassion. The woman caught in the act of adultery (John 8:1-11), the sinful woman who anointed Jesus feet with oil, (Luke 7:36-50) and the forgiveness he offered to the woman in Samaria (John 4:1-43) are only three examples of the compassion of Christ. When Jesus called Matthew to be one of his apostles he reminded the self-righteous Pharisees, "Go and learn what this means, I desire mercy, not sacrifice. For you have come to call not the righteous but sinners" (Matthew 9:13).

Jesus' compassion were shared with all; so should it be with all of us. Humbling ourselves sufficiently to demonstrate compassion in our daily lives must be a goal that we all seek. A little story helps us to understand our responsibility in demonstrating compassion toward others: There was an old man who carried a little can of oil with him everywhere he went, and if he passed through a door that squeaked, he put a little oil on the hinges. If a gate was hard to open, he oiled the latch. So he passed through life lubricating all the creaking places, making it easier for those who came after him. People called him eccentric, strange, cranky, and sometimes even harsher names. But the old man went steadily on, refilling his can of oil when it became empty and oiling the squeaky places he found. He did not wait until he found a creaky door or rusty hinge and then go home to get his oil can; he carried it with him at all times. In a similar way, we find lives that creak, squeak, and need our oil of compassion. Let us, therefore, be ready with oil can in hand, imitating the compassion, humility and reconciliation of Jesus Christ the one whose name we bear and whose example we seek to follow.

Lent 5
Hebrews 5:5-10

The Redemptive Side of Suffering

So also Christ did not exalt himself to be made a high priest, but was appointed by him who said to him, "Thou art my Son, today I have begotten thee"; as he says also in another place, "Thou art a priest forever, after the order of Melchizedek." In the days of his flesh, Jesus offered up prayers and supplications, with loud cries and tears, to him who was able to save him from death, and he was heard for his godly fear. Although he was a Son, he learned obedience through what he suffered; and being made perfect he became the source of eternal salvation to all who obey him, being designated by God a high priest after the order of Melchizedek.

"When Christ calls a person, he bids that one to come and die." These words were written by Dietrich Bonhoeffer, a well-known Lutheran pastor and theologian, in a book influential to many, *The Cost of Discipleship*, first published in 1937. Bonhoeffer lived his Christian call to holiness without counting the cost. He did what God asked of him; he was obedient to the call of God and the teachings of Christ. He followed Christ without qualification, reservation or question. He did not look over his shoulder and wonder why, but rather lived what he wrote. His discipleship, which he lived to the fullest, cost him his life.

Bonhoeffer was born in the state of Prussia in 1906 and grew up in an academic environment near the University of Berlin where his father was a professor of neurology and psychiatry. Later in his own study of theology he became interested in the historical-critical methods of Adolph von Harnack and was a disciple of Swiss theologian Karl Barth who promoted the new "theology of revelation." After completing his doctorate, Bonhoeffer in 1931 spent one year at New York's Union Theological Seminary in a post-doctorate fellowship and exchange program. Returning to Germany, he resumed duties which he had earlier begun as a pastor and writer.

In 1933, however, things changed for Bonhoeffer, the German people, and ultimately the world with the rise of the Nazi regime and Adolph Hitler. Bonhoeffer was one of the first and most vocal opponents of Hitler and his Nazi ideology of anti-Semitism. He realized that fidelity and obedience to God were paramount and he was willing to do what was necessary, even to the point of suffering, in order to maintain his obedience and fidelity to God. He knew he must oppose what was wrong. Between 1935 and 1940 Bonhoeffer headed an underground seminary for Germany's "Confessing Church," (even though it was proscribed in 1937) which led the German Protestant resistance to Hitler. He was able to continue his work as pastor and theologian in the early war years under cover as a member of the military intelligence community. Bonhoeffer believed that the root evil for many of society's problems was a lax attitude toward morality which he said was fostered by the ready distribution of "cheap grace" to members of the church. He was an ecumenist and promoted his belief in his speeches and writings. Overall, he realized his need to be faithful to principles and obedient to God and the path the Lord set for him to follow.

In April 1943 Bonhoeffer's books, essays, and talks led to his arrest for insurrection. He was ordered imprisoned, but this only strengthened his beliefs. It was at this time that he wrote his most famous work, *Prisoner of God: Letters and Papers from Prison.* Implicated in a failed July 1944 plot to assassinate Hitler, Bonhoeffer was transferred to a concentration camp in Flossenberg, Bavaria where on April 9, 1945, only days before the allied liberation of the prison, he was executed at the direct order of Hitler. Dietrich Bonhoeffer died for the Christian beliefs which formed his life; he was a martyr who never counted the cost of his discipleship and obedience to Christ.

Dietrich Bonhoeffer's willingness to suffer as a disciple of Jesus and to be obedient to the mission and message that Christ brought to the world provides an excellent example of the challenge presented by the author of the letter to the Hebrews in our second lesson today. In some ways the latter years of Bonhoeffer's life, when he stood in opposition to Hitler and his regime, were one long period of Lent, the time when he was continually tested to see how committed he was to Christ. The author of Hebrews tells us that Jesus' suffering, which we know was grave and prolonged in many ways, helped him to learn obedience. Certainly since he is God, Jesus did not need to be taught or learn anything, but as a human, like you and me, he came to realize how instructive suffering was.

When we think of the suffering of Jesus, we almost automatically turn to the crucifixion. Clearly Jesus' physical suffering at that time was severe, but he suffered in many other ways as well. He must have suffered greatly on numerous occasions when the message he sought to proclaim was rejected by his own Jewish people. As Saint John reminds us in the prologue of his gospel: "He came to what was his own, and his own people did not accept him" (John 1:11). Jesus certainly suffered at the death of his friend Lazarus. Again, Saint John tells us that upon arrival at his friend's home, "Jesus began to weep. So the Jews said, 'See how he loved him!' " (John 11:35-36). Although he predicted it, Jesus must certainly have suffered when his chosen leader, Peter, denied him three times when he needed him the most (Luke 22:54-62). Can we imagine how Jesus suffered when Judas betrayed him for thirty pieces of silver? (Matthew 26:15). Yes, Jesus suffered physically, a painful and lingering death, but his psychological pain and disappointment may have been even greater. The Lord's ability to endure is why we hear in the reading from Hebrews that Jesus became the source of eternal salvation for all who obey him. His willingness to continue on the road that his Father set out for him, to write the final chapter of salvation history, became the great example for all who would seek to follow in his footsteps. We, the contemporary disciples of Jesus, must take up the mantle and realize that through the various manifestations of suffering in our life we too will find a greater ability to be obedient to the will of God — and to do our share to build Christ's kingdom in our world.

Through Jesus' obedience to the will of his Father, the world was saved, but we, in imitation of Christ, have been commissioned through baptism to walk the Christian vocation in our time, and not looking back, but rather always continually moving forward, with the realization that suffering and pain will be part of the journey. This is certainly not an easy proposition, today especially, as contemporary society suggests that suffering should be avoided at all costs and obedience to a set of values and ideas opposed to an increasingly secular society is not a value widely sought. We certainly do not need to seek suffering, for as we all know it will come our way sooner or later. However, many today are unwilling to journey through the episodes of pain and suffering, whether physical or of another variety, because they find no value in the lessons they might learn. However, a moment of reflection will tell us that most of the important and significant lessons of life have been learned as a result of some form of suffering, whether that be failure, physical pain endured or pain given to others by our own actions or words, or even suffering humiliation before others. When things are going well we take little time to reflect upon our activities, but when suffering in its various forms comes our way, it prompts us to think more deeply and at greater length about our life, what caused the pain and what can be done to alleviate it in the future. People in the past often talked about "the school of hard knocks," the idea of learning through enduring some failure. The veracity of that statement is just as true today as it was when it was first coined.

The season of Lent should be a period when Christians take the time that is often not set aside throughout the year, to truly evaluate our spiritual lives in every aspect. Christ has called each one of us by name to be a contemporary disciple in whatever vocation has been mapped out for us. Certainly this season of grace prompts us to think more about our life of prayer, our commitment to our community of faith, our service to our brothers and sisters in physical need, and how we can do a better job to live and promote the mission and message of Jesus Christ in our world. Jesus has shown us the way in every aspect of his life. Indeed, the example that the Lord demonstrated when he walked this earth may be his greatest legacy. Today, our reading from the letter to the Hebrews, an early Christian tract that sought to strengthen the faith of its recipients and appeal to them for perseverance despite harassment from forces outside the community, challenges us during this Lent to not fear the difficulties and hurdles of life, but rather to see them as opportunities to learn important lessons while growing closer to Christ. Even though he was the Son of God, Jesus willingly entered our world, experiencing the human condition in every way, excluding sin. His obedience to God, by going forward and never hesitating to carry out his mission, despite opposition on many fronts, must be the example we follow in our lives.

The Christian life will not be easy for those who truly live it to the fullest extent. Dietrich Bonhoeffer was only one disciple of Christ, but he serves as an excellent example of someone who despite severe opposition and much suffering, both personally and psychologically, never wavered in his commitment to follow in the footsteps of Jesus. Few, if any, of us will ever be called upon to give our lives as martyrs as did Bonhoeffer, but if we are not suffering to some extent, especially these days by standing up for what we believe against the tide of secularism and in many ways anti-Christian sentiment, then we may need to rethink what we do, for we are not living the Christian vocation to its fullest. Bonhoeffer wrote, "When Christ calls a man, he bids him come and die." Let us, as Jesus says in the gospel numerous times, die at least somewhat to self during this Lenten season, so that we may learn the essential lessons of life, aid others, and most importantly bring ourselves closer to the source of life today and eternal life tomorrow.

The Cost of Discipleship

Have this mind among yourselves, which is yours in Christ Jesus, who, though he was in the form of God, did not count equality with God a thing to be grasped, but emptied himself, taking the form of a servant, being born in the likeness of men. And being found in human form he humbled himself and became obedient unto death, even death on a cross. Therefore God has highly exalted him and bestowed on him the name which is above every name, that at the name of Jesus every knee should bow, in heaven and on earth and under the earth, and every tongue confess that Jesus Christ is Lord, to the glory of God the Father.

Long ago on a high mountain top three trees were speaking about their future dreams. The first tree said, "I would really like to made into a cradle so that a newborn baby might rest comfortably and I could support that new life." The second tree looked down at a small stream that was flowing into a big river and said, "I want to be made into a great ship so I can carry useful cargo to all corners of the world." The third tree viewed the valley from its mountain top and said, "I don't want to be made into anything. I just want to remain here and grow tall so I can remind people to raise their eyes and think of God in heaven who loves them so much."

Years passed and the trees grew tall and mighty. Then one day three woodcutters climbed the mountain in order to harvest some trees. As they cut down the first tree one of the men said, "We will make this one into a manger." The tree shook its branches in protest; it did not want to become a feed box for animals. It had grander ideas for its beauty

47

but the woodcutters made it into a manger and sold it to an innkeeper in a small town called Bethlehem. And when the Lord Jesus was born, he was placed in that manger. Suddenly the first tree realized it was cradling the greatest treasure the world had ever seen. As the woodcutters cut down the second tree they said, "We will make this into a fishing boat." The tree protested, but the woodcutters did as they planned and a man named Simon Peter bought it. And when the Lord Jesus needed a place from which to address the crowds that were pressing upon him, he got into the little fishing boat and proclaimed the good news. And the second tree suddenly realized it was carrying the most precious cargo of all time, the king of heaven and earth. The woodcutters than came to the third tree and said, "The Romans are paying good money these days for wooden beams for their crosses. We will cut this tree into beams for a cross." The tree protested so hard that its leaves began to shake and then fall onto the ground, but it was cut down, nonetheless, and made into beams.

One Friday morning the third tree was startled when its beams were taken from a woodpile and roughly placed onto the shoulders of a man. The tree flinched when soldiers nailed the man's hands to the wood; the tree felt shamed and humiliated. But early on Sunday morning, as the dawn appeared, the earth trembled with joy beneath the tree. The tree knew that the Lord of all the earth had been crucified on its cross, but now God's love had changed everything. And the cross from that third tree stands tall to remind people to raise their eyes and think of the God in heaven who loves them. And did you notice, how in each case, being cut down was the price that was paid for entering into God's glory?

Today the Christian community throughout the world begins its most sacred time, Holy Week. During this special week of prayer and reflection, Christians throughout the world make their final preparations for the commemoration of the Paschal Mystery, culminating with the celebration of the resurrection of Jesus Christ. However, before we can reach the greatest event of our salvation, we must walk the road with Jesus that begins today with his triumphal entry into the city of Jerusalem. From the perspective of the synoptic evangelists, Matthew, Mark, and Luke, this is the one and only time that Jesus comes to Jerusalem, and he does so for the sole purpose of sacrificing his life so that humanity, God's greatest creation, could have the possibility of eternal life. It is, thus, extremely important that we take the time and make the effort necessary to recall the great events this week entails.

Today Jesus arrives triumphantly into Jerusalem, but we realize that the exalted "Hosannas" from the people will, in only five days, turn into cries of "Crucify him!" Saint Paul in his famous Philippians hymn, most scholars would suggest from literature of the day is not original to Paul, describes how Jesus, though God, emptied himself of his divinity to take on the human condition in all ways, except sin. He did so for the sole purpose of bringing to its climax the great story of salvation history. After the fall of Adam and Eve, God needed a plan to bring about the salvation of humanity. That plan, inaugurated with the call of Abraham, was lived day-by-day, often very unworthily, by the Hebrews during the days of judges, kings and prophets, and eventually found its apex in the life, mission, and ultimate sacrifice of Jesus on the cross. Paul describes Jesus' great humility, allowing himself to be unjustly arrested, publicly humiliated, and unmercifully crucified like a common criminal. What had Jesus done to earn such humiliation? The answer, of course, is that he had done nothing, which makes his sacrifice for unworthy humanity, who collectively have done much to grieve God, that much more remarkable.

The commemoration of Holy Week, the journey that we inaugurate this day, and Saint Paul's challenging words in his letter to the Philippians, suggest that we, as contemporary disciples of the Lord, must do what is necessary to humble ourselves, and be willing to accept difficulties, obstacles, and hurdles in life. There is, as Jesus says himself, much suffering on the way to the Father. Yet, we know in faith that if we are willing to walk the road with Jesus, to carry the crosses of our life, in the end we will achieve the goal for which we were actually sent into the world, namely to return to God in eternal life. Saint Paul, writing to his friend Timothy reminded us, "If we have died with him, we will also live with him; if we endure, we will also reign with him; if we deny him, he will also deny us; if we our faithless, he remains faithful — for cannot deny himself" (2 Timothy 2:11-13).

Yes, the Christian life will not be easy, but Jesus never promised an easy road. Quite to the contrary, he suggested just the opposite: "If any want to become my followers, let them deny themselves and take up their cross and follow me" (Mark 8:34b). Unfortunately, although the teaching of Jesus is very clear and straightforward, we don't want to accept the fact that discipleship will actually cost us something; we want a smooth, easy ride to life eternal. But the reality is that the cost of discipleship, to be a true follower of Jesus, as the famous Lutheran pastor and writer, Dietrich Bonhoeffer, reminded us in his famous book, *The Cost of Discipleship*, will indeed be high. We most likely will not suffer a martyr's death like Bonhoeffer, but if we believe that we are adequately and properly living the Christian life and have not suffered, then possibly we need to reevaluate our relationship with the Lord. Quite obviously there is no need to go looking for suffering and pain; it will come to us, often without warning, throughout our life. The question is, however, do we accept this suffering as one of the crosses sent our way, or do we seek to run away, hide, and hope that it will all go away? We simply cannot live the fantasy that indeed Christianity, if lived well, will not be a challenge. We must remember the words of the British writer, G.K. Chesterton, who once famously stated in *What's Wrong with the World*, "The Christian ideal has not been tried and found wanting. It has been found difficult, and left untried."

The great challenge presented to us by Saint Paul in his famous Philippians hymn, and the opportunity to reflect upon the great events of the week we commence today, must prompt us to look at our lives seriously and ask, are we truly willing to be a disciple of Jesus? To walk alongside Jesus and observe his great miracles, hear his teachings, and observe his triumphal entry into the holy city of Jerusalem is rather easy, for it does not cost us anything. However, for us to empty ourselves, as Jesus emptied himself, so that we might in humility serve our brothers and sisters and to realize that suffering is indeed part of the Christian life, is anything but easy. Yet, this is precisely the challenge that the Lord gives to us today. Maybe the great challenge we face is in our family, an addicted child or parent, a lack of fidelity in relationships, or financial distress. Possibly the great challenge comes in our place of work — a difficult supervisor who simply will not understand, colleagues who seem to believe that they owe little or nothing to their fellow workers, or a situation of unethical practices. Maybe the great challenge lies in our faith itself — the inability to truly believe that even in the darkest hours, with God all things are possible and solutions to life's most difficult challenges can be found.

As we commence this sacred week of prayer, let us listen well to the challenge of Saint Paul, who only echoed the words of his Lord and Savior, Jesus Christ, and truly walked the road with him. We cannot find the joy of the resurrection without passing through the pain and suffering of Good Friday. Thus, let us be that much more determined to walk the one and only road, the difficult path that leads to life. If we can, our reward in heaven will indeed be great.

Maundy Thursday
1 Corinthians 11:23-25

How Faithful Are We?

For I received from the Lord what I also delivered to you, that the Lord Jesus on the night when he was betrayed took bread, and when he had given thanks, he broke it, and said, "This is my body which is for you. Do this in remembrance of me." In the same way also the cup, after supper, saying, "This cup is the new covenant in my blood. Do this, as often as you drink it, in remembrance of me."

Mrs. Dowson stood in the doorway of Arthur's room and buttoned the cuff on the sleeve of her pink blouse. There had been a button missing but Marie had replaced it, despite all the work she had to do, the cooking, cleaning, and all the other house work. Marie was a treasure — that is how Mrs. Dowson's mother would have described her. Mrs. Dowson crossed Arthur's room to the mantel where the Seth Thomas clock was located. She tried to set the time; the clock has stopped at two o'clock. It was a lost effort, however, as the brass key which had been under the clock was missing.

"I hope you slept well, Arthur," Mrs. Dowson said. "Toward morning, I put on the light blanket and turned on the radio to listen to some music. It was an hour before I got back to sleep. "The days are longer," she told him. "You know how I like to get up with the sun in the morning. How lovely it is to hear the first bird sing. Don't you think there are more birds this year? They say that since people stopped using all those insecticides that the birds are coming back. There were some new birds at the bird bath yesterday. I should look them up in your bird book. There were some gulls as well.

Remember how the gulls used to fly off to meet the fishing boats returning to harbor. They seemed to know which boats were gutting fish and which were not.

"I used to wish you were not such an avid fisherman, Arthur. I was often lonely. Some days the ladies would josh with me and say they were golf widows but that I was a fishing widow." Mrs. Dowson began to weep, the tears running down her cheeks. "I saw you even less at home those days. It wasn't just the fishing Arthur. It was anything that attracted you, anything at all."

"No more tears, Arthur," she said finally. "You don't like tears and I've never tried to annoy you. But how long will I have to wait? You are being cruel, though you are not a cruel man. Men do what they please and get away with it. But once when I was lonely," Mrs. Dowson said, "I fell. He meant nothing to me except that he was gentle and noticed my hair and touched my face. He was there, Arthur, but God knows where you were, for days at a time."

"I atoned and God has forgiven me because God is good, but you never forgave me. It hurt your pride. I was one of your possessions that someone else had used. I guess I don't blame you, but Arthur, how long will you make me wait for a word — one word?"

Mrs. Dowson dabbed her eyes once more and then put on her gray coat. Henry was waiting with the blue Lincoln. They drove through the pylons of Auburn Cemetery. They passed many graves and Mrs. Dowson knew all the names — Henry Wadsworth Longfellow, Francis Parkman, Edwin Booth, Winslow Homer. On Orchid Path Henry stopped the car at a small mausoleum. The brass door opened easily to the key and disclosed a small space with a marble angel and a Latin phrase from Saint Paul. The chauffeur took yesterday's roses from the shelf and replaced them with a sheaf of yellow azaleas. Mrs. Dowson seated herself in the metal armchair, took off her gloves and folded her hands in her lap. "Good morning, Arthur," she said, "I am here."

Mrs. Dowson made some errors, but she was ultimately faithful to her husband, Arthur, and to God; Arthur, however, was not. Despite his infidelities and sinfulness, she remained faithful to the end, even after his death. This story serves as a good metaphor for today's Scripture lesson from Saint Paul and equally importantly, the special time we enter as Christians who recall the great events of Salvation History, the Paschal Mystery, the passion, death, and resurrection of Jesus Christ. We recall that Holy Week began last Sunday when we heard about Jesus' triumphal entry into the city of Jerusalem. We also recall what Saint Paul wrote in his Letter to the Philippians that the greeting Jesus received from the people was a lie. As Paul wrote, Jesus, although God, chose to humble himself to take on the human state, to suffer and die so that we could find eternal life. On this Maundy Thursday, when Jesus eats his Last Supper with his apostles before his suffering and death, Saint Paul, in the earliest chronological account of the institution of the sacrament of Communion, describes the fidelity of Jesus in leaving behind his presence among us. While God, like Mrs. Dowson, has ever been faithful to us, we, unfortunately too often, are like Arthur and stray away from our fidelity to God. Paul's words, however, combined with the events we commemorate, encourage us to be more faithful in our commitments, to family and work, but most especially to God.

Saint Paul's account of the events of the Last Supper precede by some ten years, we are told by biblical exegetes, the more detailed account described in the Gospel of Mark, chronologically the first of the evangelists. Thus, what Paul says is indeed important and should be recognized and appreciated by us. We are told that Jesus broke bread and offered wine as a perpetual sign of his presence with us. Moreover, we are told that we must continue this ritual, as the

Christian community has done for 2,000 years. His words ring in our ears, "Do this in remembrance of me" (1 Corinthians 11:24b). Knowing that he would die, rise and, and eventually ascend back to the Father, Jesus, in a gesture of great love and fidelity, left the world his presence among us. While he would no longer be physically present, he left himself behind in a very real way. His words have become central to Christian celebrations and serve as one of the great uniting forces in the more modern ecumenical spirit of the twenty-first century. While Christians may differ on some of the specifics associated with this sacrament, the common denominator of fidelity, namely God's fidelity to the human race, remains a rock-solid principle for all who seek to follow Jesus.

A few moments of reflection on the magnanimity of God's fidelity to humanity must prompt us to ask how faithful have we been to God and to God's people? Salvation history is replete with evidence of God's fidelity to his people. God the Father's ever-forgiving nature in the Old Testament is matched by the compassion and outreach of Jesus, his Son, to the poor and those in need. The Lenten season which now comes to a close is one, as we learned from the outset, a time for prayer, fasting, and almsgiving. It is a time given us by the church each year, to be more reflective about our life and to ask some possibly difficult and challenging questions of ourselves. Like most things in life, the daily living of our faith can become routine, mundane, and even stale. We do not take the time that is necessary to truly look at our lives and judge, without making excuses, how faithful we have been to the Christian vocation that at the time of our baptism we were called to live. Christianity lived well, especially in an increasingly more secular culture, requires that we be that much more vigilant in how we live as contemporary disciples of Jesus Christ. Thus, we must take the time to honestly examine our lives and to reflect upon our relationship with God and our fidelity to him. Although he was a pagan, we may recall what Socrates once famously uttered at his trial for corrupting youth, "The unexamined life is not worth living."

Saint Paul's description of the institution of the sacrament of Communion, where Jesus brought to an apex his consistent action of fidelity to humanity by leaving his presence among us, must prompt us to examine our lives and ask how faithful have we been? Fidelity must be found in our relationships, in marriage, family, and friendships. When we fail to be faithful and responsible to others we are acting in a way directly contrary to our Christian vocation. When we fail to give our best effort at our place of employment, if we cut corners in what we do to make things easier for ourselves, often at the expense of others, we are equally unfaithful. We live in a nation of laws and democratic procedures. If we resort to lawlessness, cheat others or think that we are righteous by carrying out merely the letter and not the spirit of the law, then we are not demonstrating the fidelity we should. If we ignore our responsibilities as citizens, yet enjoying all the privileges, we are being unfaithful. Obviously our fidelity to God must be our greatest concern. When we fail to pray each day, or to be active members of our local parish, or to meet our responsibilities to assist our brothers and sisters in distress, we are being unfaithful to God. When we think only of ourselves and our own desires, when we knowingly sin by our violation of God's law, we demonstrate infidelity once again. Since Jesus was human and thus understands the frailty of our nature, he does not expect us to be perfect. Yet, he does expect us to give our best effort. We know, by our conscience and what we feel in the depths of our heart, when we are faithful and when we are not. The choice, as always — is totally up to us. God does not place us in a straitjacket and demand obedience. Rather, he gave us free will to follow if we choose. Yes, we have a choice, but the one and only path to eternal life is clear.

As we enter this most sacred time of our Christian year, let us consider the fidelity of God toward us and ask how faithful have we been to God? Jesus' arms are lovingly outstretched on the cross just waiting for us to acknowledge our need for him and to receive his embrace of forgiveness. Let's accept his invitation to return to him with our whole heart, to recommit ourselves in fidelity, so that we can be properly prepared to celebrate the resurrection, the greatest event in Christian history, the act of fidelity that gave us the gift of eternal salvation.

Good Friday
Hebrews 10:16-25

Sacrifice Leads to Life

This is the covenant that I will make with them after those days, says the Lord: I will put my laws on their hearts, and write them on their minds," then he added, "I will remember their sins and their misdeeds no more." Where there is forgiveness of these, there is no longer any offering for sin. Therefore, brethren, since we have confidence to enter the sanctuary by the blood of Jesus, by the new and living way which he opened for us through the curtain, that is, through his flesh, and since we have a great priest over the house of God, let us draw near with a true heart in full assurance of faith, with our hearts sprinkled clean from an evil conscience and our bodies washed with pure water. Let us hold fast the confession of our hope without wavering, for he who promised is faithful; and let us consider how to stir up one another to love and good works, not neglecting to meet together, as is the habit of some, but encouraging one another, and all the more as you see the day drawing near.

In the fifteenth century, a rural village in Germany was home to a family with eighteen children. The family was poor, but despite the difficulty of making ends meet, two of the boys still held a dream, namely to pursue their talent as artists. With the financial situation bleak, the two boys came up with their own solution to the problem. They agreed to toss a coin with the loser going to the local mines to work so he could support the other while he attended art school. When the first was finished with his training, he would support the education of the other, either by sale of his art works or by going to the mines himself. Thus, one brother went off to the dangerous mines while the other went to the art academy. After four years the young artist returned triumphantly to a homecoming dinner. The artist rose from the table to drink a toast to his beloved brother for his years of sacrifice. He said, "Now Albert, it is your turn to go to the academy and pursue your dream; I will support you."

Albert sat at the table and tears began to flow down his cheeks. He began to repeat, "No, no, no." Finally Albert rose, wiped the tears from his face and holding his hands out in front of him said softly, "No, brother, it is too late for me to go. Look at what four years in the mines have done to my hands. The bones in every finger have been crushed at least once and I suffer from arthritis so badly that I cannot even hold a wine glass properly to return your toast, much less make lines on a canvas with pen or brush. No, brother, for me it is too late."

Then, one day to pay homage to his brother who had sacrificed his life for him, the great artist Albrecht Dürer painstakingly drew his brother's hands with palms together and crooked fingers pointed skyward. He called his powerful drawing simply *Hands*, but the entire world almost immediately opened its heart to the masterpiece and renamed his great work and tribute of love *The Praying Hands*.

The story of the creation of Albrecht Dürer's master etching depicts how far one man was willing to go for another. Albert Dürer's sacrifice for his brother gave the world a treasured masterpiece; Jesus Christ's self-sacrifice on the cross brought the world the one and only gift that anyone needs, the possibility of life eternal. On this Good Friday, as we commemorate how Jesus emptied himself totally, allowing himself to be unjustifiably ridiculed, beaten, and ultimately crucified, we are prompted to ask the difficult question of how self-sacrificing have we been in our lives? Do we have sufficient trust in God that if we deny ourselves, pick up our cross, and follow the Lord we will truly find eternal life, or are we constantly hedging our bets, giving some but not all to the Lord? The author of the Letter to the Hebrews both encourages and challenges us to persevere in a life of self-sacrifice, confident that God's total fidelity to us by sacrificing his only begotten Son for our sake, will lead us back home to God, if we have the courage to be true disciples.

Today's lesson from the letter to the Hebrews presents many important themes centered about the concepts of sacrifice and perseverance. As God persistently assisted the Hebrews, and manifested this fidelity through the law, so Jesus continues for the Christian community to provide a new covenant, written not on stone, but in our hearts and minds. Rather than abandoning the law, which was so central to the Jews, Jesus brings an additional part, the spirit of the law that joined with the letter of the law in the Decalogue and the 613 laws of the Hebrew Bible, presents the fullness of God's fidelity to his people. Because God is faithful he does not remember our sins, but rather provides forgiveness; all we need do is ask. For the author of this passage from Hebrews, Jesus is the great high priest to whom we can go with complete assurance that even if we have sinned, our consciences will be sprinkled clean and our sinfulness driven away by pure water. We are told that we must hold fast to the hope and faith that is so central to the Christian message. We must not waver; we must hold fast to our confession of faith. The fidelity of Jesus and his willingness to sacrifice totally for us must be the example to which we look in order to properly live our lives.

Being a person of persistent self-sacrifice is certainly one of the important qualities of a good Christian, yet in our very individualistic self-serving twenty-first century American society, it is not a value that is held in high esteem by many. We are schooled from our earliest days to do whatever is necessary to get ahead, to move past the competition, to achieve to the highest levels. The social Darwin principle of "the survival of the fittest" is alive and applicable in every day society. We are bombarded from every side with the message that we must never stop moving forward; self-sacrifice and holding back so that others may attain some element of the goods of the world is almost seen as failure. Yet, as the beautiful story of the creation of *The Praying Hands* suggests and as the words in the letter to the Hebrews clearly demonstrate, the Christian message is directly opposed to that of the world. That is certainly not new news, for to be a true Christian in today's world requires that we be countercultural, rejecting the norms of society and seeking the less traveled, but only road that leads to life eternal, the way of Jesus Christ.

Jesus' self-sacrifice on the cross is obviously an extreme example of the Christian message to aid others, but even though we may not be able or even asked to give our life in a physical sense for others, we must be willing to sacrifice, share and go out of our way for others. This is true in every aspect of our life. Families probably know this reality best. Parents are constantly sacrificing for their children. They put aside some of their own desires and at times their needs, so that their children can have a better and more productive life than themselves. Older siblings must learn this same message and act accordingly in their lives. Often when things go wrong in families, it is simply because members have forgotten the basic vocation of self-sacrifice. We get sidetracked and lose focus. When people begin to focus too much on their selves, then the balance that a family needs is compromised. Such imbalance creates instability and becomes the source of many problems.

Self-sacrifice must be a part of our work environment as well. Too often people today look at themselves as privileged, that the employer in some ways owes the employee something much more than a job and a just wage. Obviously, work is a necessary reality of our lives. As they say, money does not grow on trees and we must participate in the economy to meet our daily material needs. Yet, if we enter more fully into the daily tasks of our job, seeking to give of ourselves more fully, we will find what we do to be much more self-satisfying. Equally importantly the results that we will achieve will be greater, to the betterment of the company and our self.

As citizens of our local community, state, nation, and world — we have a responsibility toward others. This cannot be achieved without an attitude of self-sacrifice. We all enjoy great privileges of living in a land where respect for human rights, democratic process, and basic human freedoms are the norm. Yet, too often people act in a manner as if these great rights are in some way free, that there is no cost to citizenship. But such an attitude denies the reality that with all great privileges come significant responsibilities. Our responsibility will many times, if lived properly, necessitate self-sacrifice. We always want things done, but we expect the other guy to do it. The reality is, however, that we must shoulder the burden, at least in part, to get the job done. Such burdens and responsibilities will by their very nature require us to draw back and possibly not do all that we individually want to do. For the betterment of the whole, the common good, we must put our own desires on the "back burner," at least for some time, to make certain that the needs of all, or at least the majority, are served first.

Lastly and probably most importantly, a sense of self-sacrifice must be the way we live our faith. If we truly seek to be followers of Jesus, then the life he lived, and the sacrifices he made should be what we seek to emulate in our life. It's often not easy to share your faith with others, especially today when Christianity is in varied ways under attack throughout our world. Yet, it's a form of self-sacrifice to share our faith, in word and action with others. It is not easy to stand against the secular tide of our world which seems to be increasingly strong and anti-religious in its perspective. Yet, when we truly know in our hearts, and by our Christian doctrine, that certain actions of individuals and or government are completely antithetical to the message and mission of Jesus Christ, we must be willing to sacrifice ourselves in order to stand tall against such heretical ideas.

Self-sacrifice in all of its manifestations — family, work, citizenship, and faith — will by its nature be costly. We may lose a friendship or two; we may suffer some type of financial loss. Some type of opportunity that we truly desire may not come our way. However, that is precisely the message of Good Friday and our lesson from the letter to the Hebrews. Regardless of the pain, problems, or situation, we are called to persevere as people of self-sacrifice. We do so not need to be martyrs in order to demonstrate our holiness of life. Rather, we sacrifice because it is an integral part of the vocation of being a Christian. Such a life of self-sacrifice is not easy, yet it is the one and only life that will lead us back to God. Therefore, as we continue to walk this special road of the Paschal Mystery, let us see in some small way the sacrifices we make, whether they be for people, ideals or institutions, as a minor example of the sacrifice of Jesus on the cross. Jesus poured out his life so that we could find salvation; let us be willing to sacrifice ourselves in a similar way so that we can be true disciples of Christ and find the gift of eternal life, God's promise to all who believe.

Easter Sunday
1 Corinthians 15:1-11

Rising to New Life

Now I would remind you, brethren, in what terms I preached to you the gospel, which you received, in which you stand, by which you are saved, if you hold it fast — unless you believed in vain. For I delivered to you as of first importance what I also received, that Christ died for our sins in accordance with the scriptures, that he was buried, that he was raised on the third day in accordance with the scriptures, and that he appeared to Cephas, then to the twelve. Then he appeared to more than five hundred brethren at one time, most of whom are still alive, though some have fallen asleep. Then he appeared to James, then to all the apostles. Last of all, as to one untimely born, he appeared also to me. For I am the least of the apostles, unfit to be called an apostle, because I persecuted the church of God. But by the grace of God I am what I am, and his grace toward me was not in vain. On the contrary, I worked harder than any of them, though it was not I, but the grace of God which is with me. Whether then it was I or they, so we preach and so you believed.

Akron, Ohio, in 1935 was the site of what many might call a miracle. That year Bill Wilson, a former New York stockbroker, and Dr. Bob Smith, a surgeon in Akron, met. Both men for many years had been helpless and hopeless alcoholics. Their meeting, however, led to the foundation of Alcoholics Anonymous, an international organization which over the last eighty plus years has literally saved millions of lives by assisting people to realize their own brokenness and their need to seek reconciliation and assistance. In a very real way, Alcoholic Anonymous has been a source of resurrection and new life for many.

Prior to their meeting, Bill and Dr. Bob had each been in contact with the Oxford Group, a non-alcoholic fellowship that emphasized universal spiritual values in daily life. In New York under this spiritual influence and with the help of a friend, Bill W. had achieved sobriety and was able to maintain recovery by assisting others plagued by the disease of alcoholism. Dr. Bob's experience with the Oxford Group, however, had not brought him to sobriety. When the two men met, however, the effect on the doctor was powerful and immediate. Dr. Bob was brought face to face with a fellow sufferer; the encounter transformed his life. Bill told his new friend that alcoholism was a disease, a malady of mind, emotions, and body, a fact that he had only learned recently from a physician in New York. Bill's support and ideas brought Dr. Bob to sobriety; neither man ever drank again. Alcoholics Anonymous had generated its first spark of life, its first recipients of resurrection.

Bill and Bob immediately began to work with alcoholics at Akron's City Hospital. Soon after they started one patient quickly achieved sobriety leading the three to become the nucleus of the first AA group. The program grew slowly but effectively and by the fall of 1935 a second AA group was formed in New York; a third was established in Cleveland in 1939.

Alcoholics Anonymous grew through the assistance of friends, including John D. Rockefeller Jr. who became a charter board member of The Alcoholic Foundation. The publication of the book, *Alcoholics Anonymous*, and the establishment of a New York office helped spread the message. By 1950 some 100,000 recovered alcoholics could be found worldwide.

Bill W. and Dr. Bob realized their lives were out of control; they needed to forgive themselves and then find the assistance of others; they needed to find new life. In the development of Alcoholics Anonymous these two men found the anchor they needed. Their sobriety allowed them to lead millions of men and women to recovery and the restoration of their lives.

Today on Easter Sunday the Christian world celebrates its greatest event, the resurrection of Jesus Christ from the dead. There is no more central event for followers of Jesus, since through the Lord's conquest of death we, who seek to follow in his footsteps, now possess the possibility of eternal life. As Alcoholics Anonymous has almost literally brought millions of men and women from the brink of death to a renewed life in sobriety, so Jesus' resurrection brings renewal to our lives. We need not wait to our moment of death and judgment to find the fruits of this great event, for in many ways we can and may need a sense of resurrection in our daily lives. We may have to move from the throes of despair, addiction, financial failure, divorce or maneuvering through the serious illness or death of a loved one. All of these many "deaths" in our lives need the healing remedy of Christ's resurrection.

Because of its centrality, it is certainly no surprise that all four of the gospel evangelists present a clear account of the resurrection. While the gospel of Mark, the first evangelist chronologically, presents a very brief story, Matthew, Luke, and John give more full accounts, including many famous post-resurrection stories. Interestingly, however, the first written account of the resurrection actually comes from Saint Paul, as we heard in today's second lesson. Paul states, "For I handed on to you as of first importance what I in turn had received: that Christ died for our sins in accordance with the scriptures, and that he was buried, and that he was raised on the third day in accordance with the scriptures and that he appeared to Cephas, then to the twelve" (1 Corinthians 15:3-5). He goes on to say that Christ appeared to many others, and ultimately to Paul himself, even though because of his former way of life as a persecutor of Christ and his followers, he did not deem himself worthy of such an honor. Because Paul was granted this meritorious honor, he realized that it was incumbent upon him to work harder than others in his role as the apostle to the Gentiles. From his own experience, Paul understood what resurrection meant. From the perspective of Christ and his followers Paul was dead until Jesus came to him on the road to Damascus (Acts 9:1-19). Because Paul understood what it meant to move from death to life in Christ Jesus, he exhorts the Corinthians to seek a similar transformation in their own lives. For Paul the essential nature of not only the event of the Resurrection, but belief in its power to transform the lives of people prompts him to write and present this challenge to the nascent church in Corinth.

The resurrection of Jesus and the hope that it brings to the Christian community must be for all of us a source of great joy and consolation. Paul realized that without the resurrection our faith in Christ is hollow, even useless. He writes later in this same chapter 15 of 1 Corinthians (15:17), "If Christ has not been raised, your faith is futile and you are still in your sins." Fortunately, Christ did rise from the dead and, therefore, we are freed from sin and have the possibility of eternal life. But, as alluded to earlier, there is no need to wait until the time of our death to experience the power of Christ's resurrection in our lives. Indeed, Jesus' rising to new life can bring us renewal in so many ways. Along the road of life, we are often forced to negotiate numerous hurdles, obstacles, and forced to take detours that are experienced as a form of death. Loss of our job or the economic resources we need to make ends meet for our families feels like a form of death and we are often at a loss as to which way to turn. All of us will experience the tragedy of either serious illness and/or death to a member of our family, friend, or another loved one. We are uncertain how we can move forward without the presence of the departed person in our life. A certain part of ourselves has indeed died. Major disappointments in our family — an addicted member, the need for one to relocate due to job or military service, as examples, can cause significant consternation. It is through the power of the resurrection that we can discover the courage, fortitude, and perseverance to rise above the tragedy, failure, or detour to find a new life in Christ.

The great challenges of life that often lead to a form of death, events over which we have little or no control, are unfortunately at times accompanied or exacerbated by the darkness we bring upon ourselves through sin. We know the proper path we must walk, as followers of Jesus, but the power of evil is ever present and often we wilt in the present moment to temptation. Thus, we bring a form of death to ourselves by alienating ourselves from Christ. Jesus is ever faithful and, remembering the beautiful metaphor of the British writer, Francis Thompson, in his epic poem "The Hound of Heaven," never ceases to relentlessly search for our souls. Yet, we are not always as faithful. Writing to his friend Timothy, Paul proclaimed, "If we have died with him, we will also live with him; if we endure, we will also reign with him; if we deny him, he will also deny us; if we are faithless, he remains faithful — for he cannot deny himself" (2 Timothy 2:11-13). Thus, we have, through the great gift of free will, the choice to find resurrection, be reconciled to Christ, and return to a close and intimate relationship with him. However, while resurrection is Christ's gift, it must be accepted; Jesus does not place us in a straitjacket and demand our compliance or obedience. Rather, the gift of resurrection is extended; it is our choice whether or not to accept it.

Bill Wilson and Bob Smith were two down and out alcoholics who experienced through their addiction the throes of death, but fortunately for them and for millions of others, they also experienced resurrection and new life through their foundation of Alcoholics Anonymous. The organization has been a lifeline and source of renewal for so many people throughout the world. Thus, the great celebration of Christ's resurrection on this Easter day, should be a sign of hope for all who bear the name Christian. May this celebration of renewed life be for us a catalyst to seek new beginnings in every aspect of our life, with family, work, and our local community. Most especially, however, may Jesus' conquest of death renew our relationship and commitment to the Lord. May the resurrection event transform us forever.

The Transformative Power
of God

*That which was from the beginning, which we have heard, which
we have seen with our eyes, which we have looked upon and
touched with our hands, concerning the word of life — the life
was made manifest, and we saw it, and testify to it, and proclaim
to you the eternal life which was with the Father and was made
manifest to us — that which we have seen and heard we proclaim
also to you, so that you may have fellowship with us; and our fellowship is with the Father and with his Son Jesus Christ. And we
are writing this that our joy may be complete. This is the message
we have heard from him and proclaim to you, that God is light and
in him is no darkness at all. If we say we have fellowship with him
while we walk in darkness, we lie and do not live according to the
truth; but if we walk in the light, as he is in the light, we have fellowship with one another, and the blood of Jesus his Son cleanses
us from all sin. If we say we have no sin, we deceive ourselves, and
the truth is not in us. If we confess our sins, he is faithful and just,
and will forgive our sins and cleanse us from all unrighteousness.
If we say we have not sinned, we make him a liar, and his word is
not in us.*

*My little children, I am writing this to you so that you may not
sin; but if any one does sin, we have an advocate with the Father,
Jesus Christ the righteous; and he is the expiation for our sins,
and not for ours only but also for the sins of the whole world.*

The resident bishop at the Cathedral of Notre Dame in
Paris, who was known to be a great evangelist, reaching out
to cynics, unbelievers and scoffers, told the following story.
It seems that years ago there was a young man who would
daily stand outside the cathedral and shout terrible words

and derogatory slogans against God, the church, and anyone who entered the cathedral. He would call these people fools and all sorts of other names. People tried to ignore the man, but it was rather difficult.

One day the rector of the cathedral went outside to confront the man. The young man ranted and raved against everything the priest told him. Finally the priest addressed the young man. "Look," he said, "let's get this over with once and for all. I am going to dare you to do something and I bet you cannot do it." "Of course," the young man, gruffly responded, "I can do anything you propose." "Fine," said the priest. "All that I ask is that you come with me into the church and follow me into the sanctuary. I want you to stare at the figure of Christ and I want you to scream at the top of your lungs, as loudly as you can, 'Christ died on the cross for me and I don't care a bit.'" So the young man entered the sanctuary and screamed as loud as he could, while looking at the figure of the cross, "Christ died on the cross for me and I don't care a bit." The priest said, "Very good. Now do it again." And again the man screamed, "Christ died on the cross for me and I don't care a bit." "You're almost done now, said the priest. One more time."

The main raised his fist, kept looking at the statue, but the words would not come out. He just could not look at the face of Christ and say the words any more. Then, the bishop, to the surprise of all said, "I was that young man. That defiant young man was me. I thought that I didn't need God, but found that I did."

This story is apocryphal, but it is nonetheless a good illustration of how God works in our lives, transforming our hearts, even when we might not want such transformation, to the realization that we cannot live our lives without God. Too often we, sometimes unknowingly, live in darkness and we need to come to the light of Christ, knowing that he will not only lead us to the proper path, but even more important-ly, will forgive our sins and bring us to eternal life. On this second Sunday of Easter, when we bask in the light of the resurrection, our second lesson provides a similar challeng-ing message.

Saint John very clearly says that we are called to bask in the light which only God can provide. We recall from the famous creation story in the book of Genesis that God said on the first day, "Let there be light." Of course, this was the light of the sun that bathes the earth, an important function of our world to be certain, but not the critical light of which the evangelist speaks. Jesus is the true light who came to trans-form the darkness of the world, namely the absence of the full revelation of God, into the light which is the presence of God incarnate in him. We know, as well, that John tells us in the prologue of his gospel that the light which Christ brought was a stumbling block to many. As he writes, "He was in the world, and the world came into being through him; yet the world did not know him. He came to what was his own, and his own people did not accept him" (John 1:10-11). In our lesson today, John clearly says that those who choose to remain in the darkness, those who willingly reject the person and mission of Jesus, are liars and have no fellowship with the Lord. If, on the other hand, we reject the darkness and follow the light we have true fellowship with him, giving us the privilege of the expiation of our sin. Yes, Jesus will cleanse us from our sins, but we must first admit that we are indeed sinners and, therefore, in need of the redemption which Christ brought. He warns us that self-deception can easily find its way into our thoughts, words, and actions. In such a case we have abandoned the truth. If, however, we confess our sins, if we are truthful to ourselves and to God, then we will find redemption, and by extension, the eternal life which is God's promise to all who believe.

This message of Saint John meshes quite well with the theme of resurrection that we celebrate during this special time of the church year. As Jesus was transformed from death to life, so we are challenged to find a similar conversion from the darkness of sin in our life to the light of a renewed relationship with the Lord. In order to be transformed, however, we must first admit that we need God; we cannot find eternal life through our own effort. In the early fifth century this question was hotly contested between Pelagius, a British monk, and the great theologian, Augustine. Holding an exalted understanding of humanity and denying the concept of original sin, Pelagius claimed that it was possible to find salvation through one's own effort alone, thus obviating the need for Christ and his redemptive act of love on the cross. In response, Augustine totally rejected this thesis, insisting that Christians could not find life eternal without the grace of God, both to initiate and sustain one's relationship with the divine.

Although in the end Augustine won the battle, both historically and even today many would question the need for God, suggesting that one can operate and do things well using one's gift of free will in positive ways. This is precisely the temptation against which Saint John writes, insisting that we must walk in the light which only Christ can give; any other route brings darkness and is ultimately a dead-end that leads nowhere a faithful follower of Jesus wants to go. Thus, we must first understand and fully engage the reality that we need Christ. There is no option for the true believer.

Once we open ourselves to the light, seeking the way of Christ, and avoiding the darkness of error and sin, then we must move to the level of trust. Trust is something that is certainly developed over time; we cannot trust people instantaneously. Additionally, it is difficult to trust an individual with whom we have no tangible connection. Still, trust is absolutely essential in our relationship with Christ and is an integral element of our transformation and conversion. As with the challenge to understand our need for God, so too our trust in the Lord often conflicts with our own desire and belief that we can only trust ourselves. We often hear, and probably have stated more than once, "If you want to get the job done, do it yourself." Trusting another is difficult for it necessitates that we relinquish control of some action. We are always "hedging our bets," worried that if we cede control to another, the chances that we will be disappointed grow exponentially. Thus, because too often people fail to meet our expectations, we have difficulty with trust. Yet, part of the challenge of being a Christian is to place our trust in God. The author of the book of Proverbs (3:5) poignantly puts it this way: "Trust in the Lord with all your heart, and do not rely on your own insight."

If we are to achieve the conversion that the Bishop of the Cathedral at Notre Dame found in the story, the same one that John speaks of in our second lesson, moving from darkness to light, we must find trust in God. We must be patient and persistent in our trust, for God does not work on our timetable. Too often we think that God does not listen or refuses to grant our requests, but this is not the case. Jesus himself said: "Ask and it will be given you; search, and you will find; knock and the door will be opened for you. For everyone who asks, receives and everyone who searches finds and for everyone who knocks the door will be opened" (Luke 11:9-10). We will never receive a better guarantee in life.

A little story can help us to understand our need to place our trust in God. There was an expedition of world famous botanists who were exploring in the jungles of the Amazon rain forest. Their task was to note, record, and obtain samples of rare or to date unknown forms of fauna and plants. Looking into a deep ravine with his binoculars, the head of the expedition spotted a flower which, to the best of his knowledge, had never been catalogued. Wondering how he might be able to obtain a sample, he looked about and spied a young man from the jungle who was observing the scientists at work. He said to the young man, "I will give you $20 if you'll go over the side of the ravine on a rope and obtain a flower for me." Looking over the situation, the youth responded, "I will go over and get your flower but I need some help." He left the botanists, but returned five minutes later with an older man. He said, "Now I will go over the side of the ravine and get the flower for you, as long as this man holds the rope. He is my father." Can we have sufficient trust in God our Father as we have in our biological father?

Understanding our need for God and then placing our trust in the Lord will allow us to let go and allow God to transform us. In ministry it is often said, "Let me get out of the way so God can act." Indeed, his expression can be more broadly understood. If we have sufficient courage to trust God, and thus "get out of his way" and allow him to act in our lives, then the conversion and transformation we need is possible. Then and only then will we move from the darkness of error and sin into the light of the resurrection, and all the possibilities that a close relationship with Christ can bring. Yes, we need God and one another and we must trust that the Lord knows what he's doing in guiding us along the path of life. A beautiful little story powerfully demonstrates our need for God in the community of faith and what happens when we choose to "go it alone."

The pastor of a small rural parish heard "through the grapevine" that one of his parishioners was running around town saying that he no longer needed to go to church or be involved with parishioners or with God. He was content to be by himself, and encouraged others to join him. After a few weeks, as this man's mantra continued, the pastor decided to visit his recalcitrant parishioner. It so happened it was a cold winter evening and when he arrived he was warmly welcomed by the man who invited the pastor to take one of two seats in front of a roaring fire in the hearth. The two men spoke about all kinds of things, cautiously avoiding the whole issue of church attendance. Then, when there was a break in the conversation, the pastor stood up, went to the hearth and with a pair of metal tongs took one charcoal briquette from the fire and placed it on the bricks in front of the hearth. He sat down and the two men watched in silence as the one coal, over time, sputtered and eventually went out. Meanwhile, the rest of the coals, burning together, continued to heat the house. Then, after a couple of minutes of silence, the parishioner turned to the pastor and said, "Pastor, you will see me in church on Sunday."

The parishioner got the message. "Going it alone" eventually leads to a total loss of faith and death, while working with others and being engaged with God allows the fires of faith in our hearts to burn brightly. We may not need the great conversion and transformation of the Bishop in the Cathedral at Notre Dame, but all of us in some way or another need to trust God and to give our lives over more fully to him in our daily walk of faith. Let us, therefore, re-engage our absolute need for God and place our trust fully in him. If we can, indeed our reward in heaven will be great.

Easter 3
1 John 3:1-7

Bringing Hope to the World

See what love the Father has given us, that we should be called
children of God; and so we are. The reason why the world does
not know us is that it did not know him. Beloved, we are God's
children now; it does not yet appear what we shall be, but we
know that when he appears we shall be like him, for we shall see
him as he is. And everyone who thus hopes in him purifies himself
as he is pure. Everyone who commits sin is guilty of lawlessness;
sin is lawlessness. You know that he appeared to take away sins,
and in him there is no sin. No one who abides in him sins; no
one who sins has either seen him or known him. Little children,
let no one deceive you. He who does right is righteous, as he is
righteous.

In 1989, an 8.2 magnitude earthquake flattened much of
the state of Armenia and killed over 30,000 people in less
than four minutes. In the midst of the utter devastation and
chaos, a man left his wife in the security of others at home
and rushed to the school where he had taken his son that
morning, only to discover that the building was damaged
almost beyond recognition. After he recovered from the initial shock of his discovery, the man remembered a promise
he had made to his son a few years earlier: "No matter what,
I will always be there for you!" The man's eyes filled with
tears as he looked at the pile of debris that once was the
school, but despite the apparent hopelessness of the situation
the commitment he had made continued to haunt him.

The father concentrated on where his son might be in
the building, remembering where he had dropped him off

that morning. When he felt he knew the location he began to dig through the rubble. As he was digging, other forlorn parents, clutching their hearts and crying out the name of their child, tried to pull him off the pile saying, "It's too late! They are dead; you can't help them now." To each parent he only responded, "Are you going to help now?" And then he continued to dig. The fire chief of the city arrived and tried to pull him away from his effort stating, "Fires are breaking out and explosions are imminent. You are in danger. We will take care of things now. Please go home." But in response the loving father said, "Are you going to help now?" The police then came and said to the father, "You are distraught and angry, but in your actions you are endangering others. Go home; we will handle it." But again the father responded, "Are you going to help now?" No one was willing to help.

Courageously the man continued with his task, for he needed to know for himself if his son was dead or alive. He dug for 8 hours — 12 hours — 24 hours — 36 hours and then, in the 38th hour, he pulled back a huge boulder and heard his son's voice. He screamed his son's name, "Armand!" The boy called back, "Dad, it's me! I told the others here not to worry. I told them that if you were alive you would save me because you had promised, 'No matter what, I will be there for you!' You did it Dad." The boy and thirteen companions had been saved when a triangle-like wedge formed when the building collapsed. The father called his son, "Come out boy!" "No, Dad," said the son, "let the other kids out first, because I know you will get me. No matter what I know you will be there for me!"

This true account shows what one man was willing to do for another, the length of effort and the perseverance that might be necessary in order to accomplish a particularly difficult task, even when others think our efforts are useless. The father had unwavering hope that his son was alive and, thus, he would do whatever was necessary to find him. Today's second lesson from the first letter of Saint John speaks of the great privilege we have of being sons and daughters of God, a privilege that brings with it a great sense of hope. The challenge for us today is to accept our role as contemporary disciples of the Lord and to bring the hope which only Christ can bring to others that we meet along the path of life.

Saint John first describes the great privilege that we have of being children of God. It is out of God's great love for us that we are indeed his children. We are born into the world as children of our biological parents, but through baptism we become children of God, a very special privilege that, unfortunately, we often do not fully recognize or appreciate. Yet, as Saint John clearly tells us, we are God's children. If others in the world do not recognize our special status, we should not be alarmed, for the world, during his lifetime, did not recognize Jesus as anyone special. Once again we are reminded, as Saint John says in his gospel, that Christ was rejected by the very people to whom he was sent. Perceived to be a rabble-rouser, one who broke the Mosaic Law, and a person who was divisive in the Jewish community, Jesus was basically too much for the Jewish religious elite to handle. Thus, they brought about his death through crucifixion by the hand of the Romans.

The warning that the apostle presents in today's lesson is certainly something to which we can relate in our contemporary twenty-first century society. We live in an increasingly more secular community, where the values, ideas, principles of life that we espouse as Christians find fewer and fewer adherents; the voice of the Christian community is trampled down, almost silenced by a significant minority that loudly and broadly professes ideas that are almost directly antithetical to the message and mission of Jesus Christ. Thus, if we experience rejection, as John indicates, we should not be surprised. He tells us that we are indeed God's children now, but leaves it open as to what the future might hold. As he says, "What we will be has not yet been revealed" (1 John 3:2b). But we do know one thing, if we follow the path laid out to us by the Lord, namely the gospel message articulated by Christ, then we will, as the apostle says, one day be like him; we will reign with the Lord in heaven.

Importantly, therefore, John tells us that since we are children of God, even though we may be rejected by contemporary society, we must be people of hope for we are indeed in a very real way ambassadors for Christ in a society which is often occluded by the darkness of sin. Hope is an essential element of the Christian call. The efforts of the father to locate his son after the massive earthquake in Armenia could never have been accomplished if the man did not have great hope. Since we are children of God we must, therefore, be people of hope; any other response to the day-to-day difficulties of life is inconsistent with our Christian call.

When we look about and observe our contemporary world, one might ask, "How can I be a person of hope amidst a sea of despair?" The above-mentioned secularism of the world seems to grow exponentially. In increasing ways, we measure the viability and importance of an individual by the power, prestige, and material wealth an individual possesses. We see a world gripped in fear of international terrorism or how violence disrupts people's lives and innocent people die for no apparent reason. Christianity seems to be in retreat; Christians themselves are persecuted with many becoming martyrs. Families are devastated by divorce, fatherless children, or economic ruin. People seek answers to all of the various difficulties and problems through the solutions of the world and not those of God. In many ways it seems like a hopeless situation, but that is precisely the great challenge of Christianity, the trial of which Saint John speaks in today's lesson. The apostle warns us that we must avoid sin and, as best we can, the temptations and near occasions of sin that come our way. We must seek to be pure as the Lord himself is pure.

While the challenge before us may be great, we certainly have the assistance we need to find the proper path that will lead us to Christ and eternal life. We must stay attached to the life and mission of Christ. In his famous metaphor of the vine and branches, Saint John in his gospel gives the formula we need: "I am the vine, you are the branches. Those who abide in me and I in them bear much fruit, because apart from me you can do nothing. Whoever does not abide in me is thrown away like a branch that withers; such branches are gathered, thrown into the fire, and burned. If you abide in me and my words abide in you, ask for whatever you wish, and it will be done for you" (John 15:5-7).

Yes, keeping ourselves attached to the vine, Jesus Christ, the source of our spiritual sustenance, must always be primary in our mind. Every word and action of our day-to-day lives must in some way seek to help us draw closer to Christ. And we can be totally confident that the hope we hold in Christ will indeed hold true. We must recall what Saint Paul wrote to his friend Timothy: "If we have died with him, we will also live with him; if we endure, we will also reign with him" (2 Timothy 2:11b-12a). Christ will never abandon us; on the contrary he will be with us celebrating every triumph and holding our hand through every disaster of life. Recall the famous message from the popular "Footprints" poem that describes a man walking along the beach with Jesus and initially seeing two sets of footprints. Then, when life's challenges become extreme the man sees only one set of prints and fears that the Lord has abandoned him. But Jesus replies, "My precious child, I love you and would never leave you. During your times of trial and suffering, when you saw only one set of footprints, it was then that I carried you."

We have all heard the very positive message, "Hope springs eternal." Indeed the fact that we are God's children must make us men and women of great hope. We have the obligation to share this hope with others to bring a renewal, one might say a spring time of possibility, to those we meet. The Lord is counting on us to do his work in our world. A little story illustrates the point well: On the day of Jesus' ascension, his return to the glory of heaven, he was greeted by the Father and the Holy Spirit. Excited that Jesus had returned home, God asked his Son, "Was your mission completed on earth?" Jesus replied, "Oh no, not at all, but I left some capable people in charge." But God responded, "What if they fail; what if they lose heart; don't you have a backup plan?" Jesus responded, "No, Father, I have left them in charge; it is their task to complete my work."

Yes, indeed, Jesus has placed his trust in all of us; there is no backup plan. Therefore, let us be people of great hope. Armed with the reality that we are his sons and daughters, the children of God, let us boldly and proudly go forward, in hope, and do our share to build the kingdom of God in our world. God is counting on us; let us not disappoint him.

Loving Through Action

We know that we have passed out of death into life, because we love the brethren. He who does not love abides in death. Anyone who hates his brother is a murderer, and you know that no murderer has eternal life abiding in him. By this we know love, that he laid down his life for us; and we ought to lay down our lives for the brethren. But if anyone has the world's goods and sees his brother in need, yet closes his heart against him, how does God's love abide in him? Little children, let us not love in word or speech but in deed and in truth.

By this we shall know that we are of the truth, and reassure our hearts before him whenever our hearts condemn us; for God is greater than our hearts, and he knows everything. Beloved, if our hearts do not condemn us, we have confidence before God; and we receive from him whatever we ask, because we keep his commandments and do what pleases him. And this is his commandment, that we should believe in the name of his Son Jesus Christ and love one another, just as he has commanded us. All who keep his commandments abide in him, and he in them. And by this we know that he abides in us, by the Spirit which he has given us.

Vincent Capodanno was born on February 13, 1929 on Staten Island in New York. His early life was characterized by service to his family and the community where he lived. Always trying to help out, especially when difficult economic times stretched the family's budget, Vincent was the one to whom people went for many needs, for they knew that he would be present to them in every way possible. He completed his initial education and then entered Fordham

University, but God was calling him to a higher form of service and love. He decided to enter the religious formation program for the Maryknoll Missioners, a United States-based, but international organization of priests who shared God's love with those less fortunate throughout the world. He was eventually ordained a priest in 1957 and sent to an aboriginal community in Taiwan for his first assignment.

Although he had been trained in the native languages of the people he served, Father Vincent found it difficult. Nevertheless, he persevered and served as best he could. He loved the people and they loved him. After a few years, however, it became evident to him that God was once again calling him to serve in another capacity. It was the mid-1960s and the United States was becoming increasingly involved in Vietnam. Vincent asked and eventually received permission to enter the United States Navy as a chaplain. In early 1966 he was sent to Vietnam to serve with the Marines. While there, he became well known for his broad smile and his willingness to do anything that was required to meet the needs of the Marines he served. When his initial tour of duty was over, he volunteered to extend and continued serving in the country for another year. Many times he found himself in harm's way, but he never shied away from his duties.

On September 4, 1967, a large North Vietnamese force trapped a much smaller force of United States Marines and a major firefight ensued. Father Capodanno was on patrol with these Marines, something that chaplains were encouraged not to do. During the battle he moved from place to place, administering the final sacraments of the church to many dying Marines. In the process he was wounded by shrapnel in the face and lost most of one of his hands through enemy fire. Nevertheless he continued to serve. When moving toward a Navy medic who himself had been wounded, he was killed by enemy fire.

One year later in 1968, in recognition of his heroic service and his continual love for others, Vincent Capodanno, known to his friends and history as the "Grunt Padre" was posthumously awarded the Congressional Medal of Honor, our nation's highest military award. Later still, a United States naval vessel was named in his honor, the sixth ship in the history of the United States Navy named after a chaplain.

The life of Vincent Capodanno, a man of great fidelity and honor, is, I believe, a very fine example of demonstrating love through action, an idea expressed very powerfully by Saint John in today's second lesson. John tells us that we move from death to life by demonstrating love. We cannot live in both areas; either we fail to love and, therefore, find death or we demonstrate love and find life. He goes on to give the best example of love in the life and most profoundly the sacrificial death of Jesus. As difficult as it is for any of us to imagine, Jesus chose to give up his life for countless believers, all of whom were unworthy, that would seek to follow in his footsteps. But then John goes on and presents the great challenge for all of us. He puts it very clearly: "We know love by this, that he lay down his life for us — and we ought to lay down our lives for one another. How does God's love abide in anyone who has the world's goods and sees a brother or sister in need and yet refuses help?" (1 John 3:16-17). Then, using powerful words, John makes more generic his teaching and challenge: "Little children, let us love, not in word or speech, but in truth and action" (1 John 3:18).

John knew the tendency for all of us at times to deceive ourselves by thinking that we are acting in the truth of the gospel message. Therefore, he reminds us that we must look into our hearts for we know deep down, through the development of our conscience, when we are acting in love and when we are not. Moreover, we should never seek to deceive ourselves, for we are certainly not deceiving God, for he knows us better than we know ourselves. Therefore, we

87

must keep our words and actions, every endeavor of our life, close to Christ by obeying his commandments. We must follow the lead of the Holy Spirit who was sent by Christ into the world, as he promised, after his ascension, to direct us in the way to God.

Demonstrating love through our actions is certainly an integral part of the Christian life. As the life of Vincent Capodanno demonstrated, in line with the challenge in today's second lesson, we are called to carry out Jesus' directive to live for others. We recall his words: "No one has greater love than this, to lay down one's life for one's friends. You are my friends if you do what I command you" (John 15:13-14). Few if any of us will ever be required to lay down our life in a physical way for another, such as the martyrs or others who choose to die in the place of another. However, all of us are called through our Christian vocation, to sacrifice in some way so that others may be raised up. There are numerous ways that this can be done, some rather heroic, but others very ordinary, routine, and even mundane. If we have the economic resources to assist individuals, groups, or our various fraternal or religious organizations who help those in need, we are indeed living for others.

However, this idea is much broader than simply sharing our material resources. When using our talent and expertise to assist another, whether that be helping a fellow student in school who struggles in any particular subject, assisting a neighbor with a household project, or donating our professional expertise to assist individuals or possibly some community project, we are also living for others. When we take the time, that precious commodity which these days we never seem to have in sufficient supply, and utilize it to visit someone who is ill or infirmed, to run an errand for an individual who has no transportation, or to simply sit on the couch and listen to a family member, friend, or even colleague at work who wants to share some burden, we are living for others.

We have all heard the expression that we must not only "talk the talk," but also "walk the walk." If we claim the name and religion of Christian then we are not only challenged, but even mandated by the Lord to do what we can to assist others, to demonstrate love through action. Saint James makes it crystal clear that words without actions are hollow: "What good is it, my brothers and sisters, if you say you have faith but do not have works? Can faith save you? If a brother or sister is naked and lacks daily food, and one of you says to them, 'Go in peace; keep warm and eat your fill,' and yet do not supply their bodily needs, what is the good of that? So faith by itself, if it has no works, is dead" (James 2:1-17). If we say we love Christ and wish to be his disciples, then we must move to the level of action, by serving, and as necessary, laying down one's life for others. Since Jesus is no longer physically manifest in our world, we have the responsibility to act in his name. Saint Teresa of Avila, a famous sixteenth century Carmelite nun, wrote a beautiful prayer which indeed speaks to our responsibility: "Christ has no body on earth but yours, no hands no feet, but yours. Yours are the eyes with which Christ looks with compassion for the world. Christ has nobody on earth but yours." Yes, we, the Christian community, are the hands and feet, the eyes and the ears of Christ in our world. It is our responsibility to take up the mantle and to love others through action as did Jesus. Saint John's challenge in today's second lesson is indeed a great one, but we have the best example in Jesus, and, therefore, the inspiration we need to do what is necessary. Therefore, inspired by the story of Vincent Capodanno, and taking up the challenge of Saint John, let us love others through action. If we can, our reward in heaven will indeed be great.

Responding to God's Love

Beloved, let us love one another; for love is of God, and he who loves is born of God and knows God. He who does not love does not know God; for God is love. In this the love of God was made manifest among us, that God sent his only Son into the world, so that we might live through him. In this is love, not that we loved God but that he loved us and sent his Son to be the expiation for our sins. Beloved, if God so loved us, we also ought to love one another. No man has ever seen God; if we love one another, God abides in us and his love is perfected in us.

By this we know that we abide in him and he in us, because he has given us of his own Spirit. And we have seen and testify that the Father has sent his Son as the Savior of the world. Whoever confesses that Jesus is the Son of God, God abides in him, and he in God. So we know and believe the love God has for us. God is love, and he who abides in love abides in God, and God abides in him. In this is love perfected with us, that we may have confidence for the day of judgment, because as he is so are we in this world. There is no fear in love, but perfect love casts out fear. For fear has to do with punishment, and he who fears is not perfected in love. We love, because he first loved us. If any one says, "I love God," and hates his brother, he is a liar; for he who does not love his brother whom he has seen, cannot love God whom he has not seen. And this commandment we have from him, that he who loves God should love his brother also.

A long time ago there lived a little boy whose parents had died. He was taken in by an aunt who raised him as her own child. Many years later, after the boy had grown and become successful in business, he received a letter from his aunt. She was terminally ill and from the tone of her letter quite afraid of death. Thus, the man who had been raised and touched by this woman decided to write her a letter in response.

He began, "It is now 35 years since I, a little boy of six, was left quite alone in the world. You sent me word that you would give me a home and be a mother to me. I have never forgotten the day when I made the long journey of ten miles to your home. I remember being disappointed that instead of coming yourself, you sent your servant, Caesar, to fetch me. I well remember my tears and anxiety as, perched atop your horse and clinging to Caesar, we rode off to your home. Night fell before we finished the journey and as it grew dark I became more afraid. 'Do you think she will go to bed before we get there? I asked Caesar nervously. 'Oh, no,' Caesar replied, 'she will certainly be up to stay with you. When we get through these woods you will see a light shining in the window.'

"We made it to the clearing and there was the light as he promised. I remember that you were waiting in the doorway. You put your arms around me and lifted me, a tired and frightened little boy and gently took me from the horse and safely placed me on the ground. You had a fire burning and a hot supper was waiting for me on the stove. After supper, you took me to my new room. You listened to my prayers and then you waited until I fell asleep.

"You probably know why I am re-telling these events to you now. Very soon, God is going to send for you and take you to a new home. I am trying to tell you that you need not worry nor be afraid of the summons or of the strange journey or the dark messenger of death. God is love and can be trusted. God can be trusted to do more for you then you did for me so many years ago. So you can wait and not fear for at the end of the road you will find love and welcome awaiting you. And you will be safe in God's care. I will watch and pray for you until you are out of my sight. I shall also wait for the day when I will make the same journey and find you waiting for me to greet me at the end of the road.

The love of one woman for her orphaned nephew was returned years later by the young lad who had become a mature man. The demonstration of love given with an equal response of affection is found in this popular and profound scripture passage from Saint John which serves as our second lesson this week. As God has loved us into existence and given us all that we need to serve him and our fellow man, so we, in response, are called to love God by our manifestations of care for one another.

The centrality of love as a basic foundation for the Christian life should be obvious, but we need to periodically be renewed and reminded of this reality. Saint John speaks of God as love. If we love others then we know God, but if we fail to love then regardless of what we say, our actions demonstrate that we do not know God. God's love for us has been played out over the centuries through salvation history. From the time of the fall of Adam and Eve, as described in the book of Genesis, the Lord mapped out a plan whereby humanity could be restored to a proper relationship with God and have the possibility of eternal life. The Hebrew Bible presents the details of salvation history through the history of the Jews — the call of Abraham, the formation of the Jewish people, the escape from bondage in Egypt through the efforts of Moses and the establishment of the law, the formation of a nation, the stories of the judges and kings, and the plethora of prophets who were sent to guide and to warn the Jewish leaders of their need to follow God's law. Saint John tells us that the culmination, the apex of this wonderful story of God's care for humanity, is found in Jesus, his message and mission and most importantly his sacrificial death that atoned for the sins of humanity for all time, past, present, and future.

The great love that God has shown for us, however, must find reciprocation in our actions. As the man wrote to his aunt as a way of responding to the love she had given him as a child, so must we respond to God's love by our words and actions toward others. Saint John is very clear, "Beloved, since God loved us so much, we also ought to love one another. No one has ever seen God; if we love one another, God lives in us and his love is perfected in us" (1 John 4:11-12). John tells us that if we say we love God but ignore our brother and sister, then we are liars. Our love must be universal; we cannot discriminate. It is through our love for our brothers and sisters that we find the unifying glue which holds the Christian community together. We need God and we need one another.

Our response to the God who first loved us is not simply a proposition or invitation, but rather a requirement for those who truly want to follow Jesus and be one of his contemporary disciples. Again John very clearly states, "Those who do not love a brother or sister whom they have seen, cannot love God whom they have not seen" (1 John 4:20b). God has implanted inside each one of us his Spirit. Thus, if we fail to love, then we are not only frustrating the Spirit, but acting in a way completely contradictory to the vocation to which all God's children are called. While what we do on a day-to-day basis will certainly vary, the common unifying feature must be our willingness to demonstrate love in response to God who first loved us, unworthy though we be in many ways.

God can rightly expect us to manifest love in our daily lives, but as with many expectations from the Lord, the challenges we face in our contemporary society to be Christlike are indeed many and significant. Competition is certainly a significant obstacle toward universal love. In our first-world society we are schooled from youth to be competitive in every aspect — the athletic field, the boardroom, our social life. There are certainly times and situations where we absolutely need to put our best foot forward, whether that is the competitive market of employment, entrance to institutions of education, or sports. However, the tendency is to "run over" the competition with little concern, feeling that it is the survival of the fittest is indeed strong. Social Darwinism is indeed alive and well.

Another challenge to universal love is our desire to be labeled successful and important in our world. It is unfortunate, but we all know it is true that largely we mark the success and importance of people in our world by the amount of economic resources, power, and prestige that a person possesses. In the process of gathering these commodities, we often lose our community spirit and the love that must unite us professing, "It's every man for himself. I cannot be concerned with my brothers and sisters, but rather, must push ahead regardless of the situation." Rather than practicing love, we find ourselves at odds with others. We protect our own territory and person at all costs.

Secularism and the movement away from basic Christian values is a third challenge that seeks to insulate us from love. Society sees solutions to all difficulties in the world and what it offers. Indeed, there are many temptations to find easy fixes and immediate answers to the various challenges and problems we face in life. We want instant results and answers for all things; we are unwilling to wait. At the first sign of physical pain we go to the medicine cabinet and find some "solution." When challenges come in our relationships we seek an "easy out," rather than working through the situation to find a common solution. The quick-fix remedies that the world so readily promotes may temporarily stop the bleeding, but they serve only as a band-aid where stitches are necessary. It is through the love of God, manifest in our love for our brothers and sisters, that we will ultimately find the answers to the difficulties, hurdles, and various obstacles of life that come our way. God has loved us by giving us life, faith, and the sacrifice of his only begotten Son. Let us, therefore, renew our commitment to love others as God has loved us. Let us respond to God's love for us and be confident that through our actions and words, we will find favor with the Lord, and one day eternal life with all those who believe.

Following God's Plan

*Everyone who believes that Jesus is the Christ is a child of God,
and everyone who loves the parent loves the child. By this we
know that we love the children of God, when we love God and
obey his commandments. For this is the love of God, that we keep
his commandments. And his commandments are not burdensome.
For whatever is born of God overcomes the world; and this is the
victory that overcomes the world, our faith. Who is it that overcomes the world but he who believes that Jesus is the Son of God?
This is he who came by water and blood, Jesus Christ, not with the
water only but with the water and the blood.*

Once upon a time, long, long ago, a young man decided to become a saint. He left his home, family, and possessions, sold everything he owned, and gave the money to the
poor. He walked off into the desert to find God. He walked
through the desert sands until he found a dark cave. "Here,"
he thought, "I will be alone with God. Nothing can distract
me from God." He prayed day and night in the dark cave, but
God sent him great temptations. He imagined all the good
things of life and wanted them desperately. However, he was
determined to give up everything in order to have God alone.
After many months the temptations stopped and Saint Anthony of the Desert was at peace having nothing but God.

According to the legend, one day God came to Anthony and said, "Leave your cave for a few days and go off to
distant town. Look for the town shoemaker. Knock on his
door and stay with him for some time. The holy hermit was
puzzled by God's command, but left the next morning as he

was directed. He walked all day across the desert sands. By nightfall he had come to the village and, inquiring with the local people, found the home of the shoemaker. He knocked on the door and a smiling man and his wife opened the portal and welcomed him. "Are you the town shoemaker?" Anthony asked. "Yes, I am," the man answered. He noticed how tired and hungry the hermit looked and, thus, he invited him into his modest house. "You need something to eat and a place to rest," said the shoemaker. He and his wife prepared a fine meal for Anthony and gave him a clean and comfortable bed in which to sleep.

The hermit stayed with the shoemaker and his family for three days. He asked many questions about their lives, but did not reveal much if anything about himself, even though the couple was very curious about his life in the desert. The three talked a lot and in the process became good friends. After three days, Anthony bid the couple goodbye. He walked back to the cave wondering why God had sent him to visit the shoemaker and his family. When Anthony arrived, God asked him, "What was the shoemaker like?" "He is a very simple man with a lovely wife who is pregnant. They seem to love each other very much. He has a small shop where he makes shoes and he clearly works very hard. They have a simple house and they give money and food to those who have less than they have. He and his wife believe very strongly in you and pray at least once a day. God listened carefully and responded, "You will be a great saint, Anthony, but so too will the shoemaker and his wife."

What does it mean to be a true follower of Jesus Christ; what is the vocation of a true believer? The little story indicates and Saint John in our second lesson today tells us that by love of neighbor and service toward others we demonstrate our love for God and are, thereby, acting as his contemporary disciples. There are many vocations that reach the destination of life with God, that is being a contemporary saint and attaining salvation, but there is only one common path. It is our faith that keeps us on track and will in the end conquer the world.

Saint John presents a very comforting but, at the same time highly challenging message. He begins by telling us that those who believe in Jesus have been born of God. Through baptism we have been enlightened and given the privilege of walking in the footsteps of the master. Our membership as sons and daughters of God is manifest most strongly, the apostle says, by the love we have for God, as manifest in our maintenance of the commandments. For John, the commandments are not simply the famous Decalogue from chapter 20 of the book of Exodus, but equally if not more importantly the message of Christ as articulated in the gospels. While the message of Jesus is expressed in many ways, we must recall the Lord's response when asked, " 'Teacher, which commandment in the law is the greatest? He said to him, 'You shall love the Lord your God with all your heart, and with all your soul, and with all your mind. This is the greatest and first commandment. And the second is like it: 'You show love your neighbor as yourself' " (Matthew 22:36-39). Commonly known, we all know, as the golden rule. Jesus synthesizes his teaching and commandments in a way that is understandable to all. We are told that his commandments are not burdensome, but rather it is through our faith that we hold fast to this basic edict of the Lord. If we can, then Jesus suggests we will conquer the world.

The message that we are God's children, and knowing that doing his will brings us to salvation is comforting, but it is simultaneously extremely challenging. To be a contemporary disciple, to follow God's plan as we best understand it, challenges us in at least two significant ways. First, we must always remember how radical the message and mission of Jesus has always been. There is no question that, from the Jewish perspective, Jesus was very much a renegade in his society. He turned everything upside down taking what was normal and acceptable and replacing it with ideas that, at the time, were deemed unacceptable. When he told the story of the Good Samaritan (Luke 10:25-37), making the upstanding members of Jewish society, namely the priest and Levite, the villains, and the Samaritan, the most despised population in Hebrew society as the hero, he placed the virtue of compassion over adherence to the law, and thereby insulted the Jewish ruling elite. When he readily associated with lepers, drove demons from Legion, and allowed a hemorrhaging woman to touch him, thereby making himself ritually impure and suggested that such actions were proper, people were taken aback. When Jesus broke the Sabbath law and suggested that "The Sabbath was made for humankind, and not humankind for the Sabbath, so the Son of Man is Lord even of the Sabbath (Mark 2:27) he claimed authority far beyond the Law. Jesus turned everything on its head, saying the last will be first and the first will be last, that the exalted will be humbled and the humbled will be exalted.

Indeed, the radical nature of Jesus' teaching during his day is found in our contemporary world as well. Jesus' value system that exults humility, promotes outreach to the lowly and marginalized of society, offers compassion over tradition and rote formulations of law, and suggests that simplicity must always trump extravagance, does not, unfortunately, attract people today. Rather, today our value system is measured through the trifold acquisition of power, wealth, and prestige. In many ways, twenty-first century society, as far as its general orientation is concerned, is similar to the way humanity has operated from the beginning. Thus, today, as in the past, following the radical nature of the message and mission of Jesus is indeed a challenge.

The second great challenge is following Jesus' "golden rule," and showing love for ourselves. Christians of all types, even if they are not "churchgoers" have little or no problem loving God. The difficulty, however, arises in loving neighbor and ourselves. We are told that we must love others as we love ourselves, but this, quite obviously, necessitates that we have a positive impression, respect for, and love of ourselves. Unfortunately, many people today have a very poor self-image. Whether literally or proverbially, they look in the mirror and say, "I am not smart enough, attractive enough, athletic enough, or socially outward enough, to be loved." We look down on ourselves. We seem to have forgotten that, as the book of Genesis states, we are made in the image and likeness of God. We are fallible, incomplete, and sinful, but since we have the mark of God in our creation, we are indeed good and lovable, by God first as our creator, and then by ourselves and others. We must make this initial hurdle of loving ourselves before we can ever properly love others. Certainly, the challenge to love others is great as well. At times, people can be a trial, especially if their actions are destructive or hurtful to us, but Jesus always sought to find the "golden nugget" inside each person, that God element. This is our challenge as well. It is rather easy to love those who love us, but how difficult to love those who make our day-to-day life more difficult. Thus, the challenge to carry out the golden rule of Jesus is indeed significant.

Saint John's words of comfort and challenge, of loving God and our neighbor by following the Lord's commands can, as demonstrated by the little story, be lived out day-by-day in many ways; there is no single vocation to finding the path to Christ. Some of us, like Saint Anthony, will be the subject of future history books; some people will be well known in the community for who they are, the position they hold, or the things they have done. Most of us, however, will be, as they say "ordinary Janes and Joes," like the shoemaker and his family, hard-working people who raise and educate our children, work diligently 8 to 5 Monday through Friday, make a contribution to our community, and worship with a community of faith on Sundays. The one and only thing that is essential is that we bring our faith to whatever it is we do on a daily basis. If we bring our faith, we will indeed show our love for God and God's people. We must manifest in word and action the teachings and mission of Jesus Christ to all with whom we have contact on a daily basis. This is the life of discipleship to which, as Saint John indicates, we have all been called.

The privilege of being a contemporary disciple of Jesus necessitates, as do all great privileges, significant responsibility. We simply cannot shirk the task we have been given by the Lord to further his mission in our world. The challenge will indeed be great, but we have all of the gifts and talents we need to go forward and minister in Christ's name to others. We will undoubtedly find opposition, but then Christ was opposed by the very people to whom he was sent, his Jewish brothers and sisters. And we must recall his exhortation when fear of opposition may have inhibited his apostles and disciples from going forward: "In the world you will face persecution. But take courage: I have conquered the world!" (John 16:33). Let us, therefore, go forward as contemporary disciples of Christ, and do what we can to complete our Master's work. We may be CEOs, medical professionals, teachers, office workers, or students. The role we play is not important in God's sight, but remaining faithful to the task and to God's commandments is essential. We march forth in his name. Let us be confident that he walks with us every step of the way, to the heights of triumph and the valleys of defeat, but ultimately along the one and only path that leads to salvation and life eternal.

Ascension of Our Lord
Ephesians 1:15-23

Living in Hope

*For this reason, because I have heard of your faith in the Lord
Jesus and your love toward all the saints, I do not cease to give
thanks for you, remembering you in my prayers, that the God of
our Lord Jesus Christ, the Father of glory, may give you a spirit of
wisdom and of revelation in the knowledge of him, having the eyes
of your hearts enlightened, that you may know what is the hope
to which he has called you, what are the riches of his glorious
inheritance in the saints, and what is the immeasurable greatness
of his power in us who believe, according to the working of his
great might which he accomplished in Christ when he raised him
from the dead and made him sit at his right hand in the heavenly
places, far above all rule and authority and power and dominion,
and above every name that is named, not only in this age but also
in that which is to come; and he has put all things under his feet
and has made him the head over all things for the church, which
is his body, the fullness of him who fills all in all.*

Once there was a village with a chief who had three
sons, each of whom possessed a special talent. The oldest
was skilled in his ability to raise and care for olive trees.
The second was a shepherd, but when the sheep got sick, he
possessed special abilities to make them well. The third son
was a great dancer. When there was a string of bad luck in
his family or in the village or if anyone needed some cheer
or hope added to their lives, he would dance and bring them
joy.

One day the father told his sons that he had to go on a
long journey. He instructed them, "My sons, the people of
the village will be depending on you to help them. Each of

you has a special talent, so while I am gone I expect you to use your gifts well and wisely, so that upon my return I will find our village more happy and prosperous then it is today." He embraced his sons and then left on his journey.

For a few months things went quite well in the village, but then came the cold winter with its snow, winds, and assorted problems. First the buds on the olive trees shrank and cracked and it would, therefore, be a long time before the trees would recover. The village, because of the extremely long winter ran out of firewood, so the people began to cut down the trees and in the process stripped the village bare. Even though the first son did not want to see the trees cut down, he knew that the villagers needed heat to survive, and so he began to help them make firewood from the olive trees. Then the snow and ice made it impossible for traders to come up the river and negotiate the mountain passes. Food was scarce. So the villagers said, "Let us kill the sheep and eat them so we will not starve to death." The village chief's second son refused for a time but eventually gave in to the villagers' demands. He said, "What good will it do to spare the sheep only to have the villagers perish?"

In this way the villagers had just enough firewood for their fires and food for their tables. But the horrible winter had broken the people's spirit. They began to think that things were really much worse than they were and many began to lose hope. This belief was so strong that family by family, they began to desert the village in search for a more hospitable environment.

As spring came, the icy grip of winter began to loosen and at the same time the chief of the village returned, only to find smoke rising only from his own chimney. "What have you done?" he asked his sons when he reached his village. "What has happened to the villagers?" "Oh, father, forgive me," said the eldest son. "The people were freezing and begged me to cut down the olive trees and so I did. I gave away my talent. I am no longer fit to be an orchard keeper." "Don't be angry, father," said the second son. "The sheep would have frozen anyway, and the people were starving and thus I sent the herd to slaughter." The father understood and said, "Don't be ashamed my sons. You did the best you could and acted rightly and humanely. You used your talents wisely in trying to save the people. But, tell me, what has become of them. Where are they?" The two brothers fixed their eyes on their younger brother who said, "Welcome home, father. Yes, it has been a hard winter. There was little to eat and little firewood for heat. I thought it would insensitive and improper to dance during such suffering. Besides I needed to conserve my strength so that I could dance for you when you came home." "Then dance, my son," said the father, for the village is empty and so too my heart. Fill us with joy, courage, and hope once again. Yes, please dance!" But when the third son made ready to dance he grimaced and fell down. His legs were so stiff and sore from sitting that they could no longer be used for dancing. The father was so sad that he could not even be angry. He simply said to his youngest son, "Ours was a strong village that could have survived the want of fuel and food, but it could never survive without hope. And because you failed to use your talent wisely and well, our people gave up what little hope they had. So now what? The village is deserted and you are crippled. Your punishment has already fallen upon you." With that he embraced his two elder sons and wept.

The story of the village chief and his three sons illustrates in a profound and powerful way the contrast between those who bring hope in a difficult situation and those who do not. On this the feast of the Ascension of the Lord, we are provided in our second lesson from Saint Paul a positive message and challenge to be hope-filled people as true disciples of Jesus Christ. Jesus' return to the Father brought hope to Paul, which he shares with the Ephesians. We, in a similar way, as contemporary disciples of Christ must be equally filled with hope, proclaiming it by the actions and words of our life, bringing light to an often occluded and dark world.

Saint Paul knew this community of faith quite well as he spent significant time in Ephesus. The Acts of the Apostles (chapters 19 and 20) speak of Paul preaching to this community for some two years during his third missionary journey. Many scholars suggest he was also imprisoned there and while in jail penned some of his famous letters. He was forced to confront soothsayers and magicians, many of whom were operating from the temple of the Mother Goddess Artemis, who was a central deity for the Ephesians and many other people in the region.

Utilizing his normal pattern for letters, Paul initiates his message to the Ephesians by proclaiming his thanksgiving for the great faith they have demonstrated in holding fast against the secular and polytheistic environment in which they live. Paul is especially grateful that the initial message he proclaimed has taken root and is beginning to sprout new growth. His hope for the people is that they will grow in wisdom and knowledge of Christ as they come to understand more fully and completely the revelation which Paul has shared with them.

Paul then moves to the centerpiece of his great prayer, challenging the Ephesians to have the hope to which they have been called by Christ through faith. Rather than placing their confidence, faith, and hope in Artemis and the polyvalent hierarchy of gods and goddesses in the Greek pantheon, or in the secular enticements of the world, Paul maintains that true hope and faith can only be found in one's relationship with Jesus. Paul suggests that such hope must be the one and only avenue of trust that the Ephesians follow. They can be confident of their hope and belief in Christ since God has given Christ the authority that all is subjected to him. As Paul puts it, "And he has put all things under his feet and has made him the head over all things for the church, which is his body, the fullness of him who fills all in all" (Ephesians 1:22-23). Paul realizes that this challenge is significant, and that it will not be easy for the fledgling Christian community to hold fast in faith and hope in the message and mission of Jesus, especially in the highly charged polytheistic world of Ephesus. Yet, the apostle equally believes that, despite the challenge, the Ephesians are up to the task and can maintain hope in Christ and be models of the Christian message to others.

The story of the village chief and his sons, the message of Saint Paul, and certainly the celebration of Christ's Ascension prompt us to reconsider how committed in hope are we in our present-day situation. Quite obviously the world is often challenging. We have all experienced many instances when problems, detours, and various obstacles of life place a pall of darkness over our lives. Instances of ill health or death with family members and friends, family challenges such as wayward children, addictions or divorce, or financial crises force us to seek answers. The remedies and solutions of the world are readily apparent, tangible, and seem to provide instant fixes to difficult problems. Quite obviously pragmatism in today's world necessitates that we use the avenues and opportunities provided by society to help us in resolving our difficulties, but too often we forget, that for a Christian, the ultimate challenge of hope and faith must be found in Christ. If we allow the Lord to operate in our life, we will find the solutions we need.

The equally important and possibly in some cases even more important challenge is for us to be bearers of hope to others. This is the message the village chief sought to communicate to his sons and what Paul drives home in his prayer in today's second lesson. The two older sons in the story did what they could to maintain hope in a very practical way. The third son, however, had an even greater task in some ways. He was not given control of a material substance to meet the practical needs of the people, but he was given the ability to fill the people with hope. His failure led to the loss of the village and the great disappointment of his father. Paul wants the nascent Christian community in Ephesus to be bearers of hope, to bring the message of Christ to others. Their example of faith and hope in Christ, it is the apostle's message and desire, that will bring others into the fold.

The message of the story and the message of Paul are equally valid today. We look around, read the papers, listen to the news on radio or television and hear very little good news. Whether it is the death of innocents through violence or war, catastrophic loss of life or economic prosperity through natural disaster, the fear of international terrorism, or a more personal challenge in our family or work environment, today's society presents numerous challenges to being people of hope. Yet, that is precisely the great challenge. Jesus' conquest of death and ultimate ascension to heaven proves that the Christian message of hope is not only valid, but can and will bring answers to the multiple questions and significant challenges of our societal and personal lives. We must avoid the temptation to "go with the flow," compromise who we are and what we believe, and bend to the world and its answers. Our task, as contemporary disciples of Jesus, is to listen to his apostle Paul and realize that ultimately our hope can only be found in the Lord. The author of the book of Proverbs (3:5) is very clear: "Trust in the Lord with all your heart, and do not rely on your own insight."

Thus, as we celebrate the hope that Christ brings in his return to the Father, let us be hope-filled in our lives. May we always be confident that if we can maintain our relationship with the Lord, and through our words and actions help others to find hope we too will find our own place at the heavenly banquet and enjoy the great victory of Christ, namely eternal life, God's gift to all who believe.

The Power of Belief

If we receive the testimony of men, the testimony of God is greater; for this is the testimony of God that he has borne witness to his Son. He who believes in the Son of God has the testimony in himself. He who does not believe God has made him a liar, because he has not believed in the testimony that God has borne to his Son. And this is the testimony, that God gave us eternal life, and this life is in his Son. He who has the Son has life; he who has not the Son of God has not life. I write this to you who believe in the name of the Son of God, that you may know that you have eternal life.

The famous inventor, Thomas Alva Edison, discouraged his friend, Henry Ford, from pursuing his fledgling idea of a motorcar. Convinced of the worthlessness of the project, Edison invited Ford to come and work for him. Thankfully, Ford remained committed to his idea and tirelessly pursued his dream. Although his first attempt resulted in a vehicle without a reverse gear, Ford knew he could make it happen. And, eventually he did.

"Forget it," the experts advised Madame Marie Curie. They agreed that radium could not exist. However, Marie insisted, "I know radium is a real element. I can make it happen." And she did.

Let's not forget the Wright Brothers either. Journalists, friends, specialists, and even their father laughed at the folly of their idea for an airplane. "What a silly insane way to waste money," Orville and Wilbur were told. Others jeered, "Leave flying to the birds." "Sorry," the brothers replied,

"We can make it happen." As a result, a place called Kitty Hawk, North Carolina became the setting for the launching of their "ridiculous" idea.

Finally, consider the plight of Benjamin Franklin. The next time you marvel at the modern conveniences we take for granted — television, computers, air-conditioning, stereos, kitchen blenders, and so on, all of which work by simply plugging them into an electrical wall outlet, remember Franklin and his experiments with electricity. Franklin was admonished to stop his foolish experiments with lightning. What an absurd waste of time! Why, nothing could outdo the oil lamp. Thank goodness, Franklin knew he could make electricity happen. And he did!

All of these short vignettes describe stories of famous people who were committed to their beliefs; they were convinced that if they moved forward, disregarded the many naysayers around them, and had sufficient confidence and courage — they could achieve their goals. In a similar way, Saint John closes his first letter to the Christian community, and we close the Easter season, by hearing the message of our need for belief, confident that if we hold fast — we will be led to salvation, God's promise to all who believe.

Saint John's message of belief is presented through the vocabulary of testimony. He says that while we are surrounded by human testimony, the word of God is greater. God the Father has spoken to his son Jesus, who in turn has presented his word to the world during his public ministry. But there is more — Jesus testifies through his actions, the example he has given. Christ stood tall against the forces of evil present in his day; he never backed down from the challenges that his opponents put before him. When he was challenged concerning his association with the poor, lowly, and outcasts of society, he responded, "Those who are well have no need of a physician, but those who are sick. Go and learn what this means, 'I desire mercy, and not sacrifice.' For I came not to call the righteous, but sinners" (Matthew 9:12b-13). John tells us that Jesus' testimony has been written on the hearts of believers. Thus, believers are given the great privilege of not only possessing the testimony, but equally if not greater, the responsibility to witness to the message of that testimony in society. Christ's message is universal and, thus, John excoriates those who choose not to believe in God, calling them liars, for indeed the power and presence of God are made available to all.

The power and privilege of belief provides another very special and important gift, the rationale for our presence in the world itself, the goal of eternal life with God. John says that we have been given eternal life through the teaching and mission of his son, Jesus. Thus, all who believe and profess Jesus as Savior and Lord will find life; those who do not will lose the gift God has provided. The apostle closes this section of his letter by initiating the epilogue to his message. He says that he writes to those who believe in the name of Christ so that they may understand and experience eternal life. Like Jesus, John wants all to be saved; he desires to seek out the lost and provide the message that will bring both the faithful and those who are non-believers back to God.

John's message provides both comfort and challenge for all who believe. In a world that is filled with uncertainty, numerous problematic situations, many manifestations of injustice, and a rising level of secularism, it is certainly comforting to know that our belief in Christ and faith in his mission and message will not be forgotten. The guarantee of which John speaks, in his reformulation of the same promise articulated by Jesus in the gospels, can relieve much heartache and calm our beleaguered and weary souls. Battered and bruised by the world in which we live, Christians need this great message of hope, the assurance that our belief will lead us home to God.

The great challenge, of course, is for believers to maintain and actually profess their belief in the aforementioned environment which seeks to negate the ideas and teachings, namely the testimony, of Christ. To truly walk in the footsteps of Christ, to be a true follower and believer, a contemporary disciple, necessitates that we live in a manner contrary to the prevailing "wisdom" of society. We must be, in other words, counter cultural. When society suggests that we must follow a manner of life and profess the "truths" that the majority hails as normative, we must have the courage of our convictions to stand against the tide. When we encounter those who question or even ridicule basic Christian values, which have stood the test of time for 2000 years simply because a vocal portion of society has grabbed the spotlight and altered the thinking of many, we must have sufficient backbone to say, "No!" In other words, we must be truly committed Christians.

While history and current events are constantly being scrutinized and interpreted, it is clear that our first-world society has moved far from and, therefore, threatens the basic values and teachings of Jesus Christ. It is incumbent, therefore, upon those who are marked with a sign of faith, the baptized, to truly manifest their faith, in word and deed. Bucking the system and being counter cultural, will unfortunately, probably not draw many friends to our side; in fact, it may even create some enemies. But we must realize that Christ's message has been rejected from his time forward. Christians have always felt opposition, but it was the courage and conviction of people like Saint John, the other apostles, and the countless numbers of faith-filled Christians over the centuries, who with courage and strength continued to proclaim the truth. We will probably not be hauled into court, stoned or martyred, as were many of our predecessors in the faith, but if we do not suffer at least in part for the faith we share, then most probably, especially considering the world in which we live, we are not living our faith to the degree that the scriptures mandate. Christ went to the cross, not because he had committed any capital crime, but rather because some of the claims he made, and the actions he performed were simply intolerable to the Jewish ruling elite. Jesus was, in many ways, a nuisance who needed to be removed. We in our own way today should be a nuisance, at least to the extent that we refuse to be silenced, but speak freely and fully what we truly believe and to fortify our words with consistent actions.

It is true, the message of Saint John provides great comfort, but with such comfort and privilege incurs significant responsibility. We must live our belief as committed Christian men and women. An anecdotal story demonstrates our challenge. One day a businessman was interviewed by a reporter. He began by asking, "What is your occupation?" The man responded, "I am a Christian." The reporter, sensing that the man did not understand the question, again asked, "I mean, what is your job; what do you do?" Again the reply from the businessman was, "As I told you, I am a Christian." Obviously perturbed and flustered, the reporter continued to press the man: "You do not understand; what you do for a living?" "Listen!" My full-time job is to be a Christian," said the businessman, but "I own a furniture store to pay the bills."

Christianity is indeed a full-time job, as they say today a 24/7 proposition. We cannot be Christians only when we pray in private or attend public services at our local parish. True Christian commitment means that our beliefs must be readily apparent, transparent as they say these days, to everyone. All people, not only those that we know, but even strangers, should by the words they hear from our lips and the actions of our lives, be able to know with certainty that we are contemporary disciples of Jesus. Yes, we will fail; we are certainly imperfect. But therein lies the great challenge.

Are we ready to take up the mantle, be counter cultural despite the possible costs and provide clear evidence of our belief in the mission and message of Jesus? The message of Saint John in today's second lesson is one of comfort and challenge, but we can always recall Jesus' words of encouragement, "Remember, I am with you always, to the end of the age" (Matthew 28:20b). Let this be our consolation and our hope as we strive daily to live the life to which we have all been called, a life that will involve some suffering, pain, and several detours, but one which, in the end, will bring us to Christ and life eternal.